A Clinician's Guide to Dream Therapy

A Clinician's Guide to Dream Therapy demystifies the process of working with dreams by providing both a grounding in the current science of dreaming as well as a simple, practical approach to clinical dream work.

In addition to a survey of the current science and neuroscience of dreaming, this book includes clinical examples of specific techniques with detailed transcripts and follow-up commentary. Chapters cover how to work with PTSD nightmares and how to use experiential dreamwork techniques drawn from current neuroscience to engender lasting change. Readers will be able to discuss their clients' dream material with confidence, armed with an approach that helps them collaboratively tap into the inherent power for change found in every dream.

Backed by research, common factors analysis and neuroscience, the approaches described in this book provide a clear map for clinicians and others interested in unlocking the healing power inherent in dreams.

Leslie Ellis is an author, teacher and psychotherapist with a lifelong interest in dreams. She is a leading expert in the use of somatic approaches in psychotherapy and she specializes in teaching focusing for dreamwork, and treatment of complex trauma. For more information, go to www.drleslieellis.com.

A Clinician's Guide to Dream Therapy

Implementing Simple and Effective Dreamwork

Leslie Ellis

Routledge
Taylor & Francis Group

NEW YORK AND LONDON

First published 2020
by Routledge
52 Vanderbilt Avenue, New York, NY 10017

and by Routledge
2 Park Square, Milton Park, Abingdon, Oxon, OX14 4RN

Routledge is an imprint of the Taylor & Francis Group, an informa business

© 2020 Taylor & Francis

The right of Leslie Ellis to be identified as author of this work has been asserted by her in accordance with sections 77 and 78 of the Copyright, Designs and Patents Act 1988.

All rights reserved. No part of this book may be reprinted or reproduced or utilised in any form or by any electronic, mechanical, or other means, now known or hereafter invented, including photocopying and recording, or in any information storage or retrieval system, without permission in writing from the publishers.

Trademark notice: Product or corporate names may be trademarks or registered trademarks, and are used only for identification and explanation without intent to infringe.

Library of Congress Cataloging-in-Publication Data
Names: Ellis, Leslie (Leslie Anne), author.
Title: A clinician's guide to dream therapy : implementing simple and effective dreamwork / Leslie Ellis.
Description: New York, NY : Routledge, 2020. | Includes bibliographical references and index.
Identifiers: LCCN 2019015180 (print) | LCCN 2019016887 (ebook) | ISBN 9780429001215 (E-book) | ISBN 9780367029135 (hardback) | ISBN 9780367029159 (pbk.) | ISBN 9780429001215 (ebk)
Subjects: | MESH: Dreams–psychology | Psychotherapy
Classification: LCC BF175.5.D74 (ebook) |
LCC BF175.5.D74 (print) | NLM WM 460.5.D8 | DDC 154.6/3–dc23
LC record available at https://lccn.loc.gov/2019015180

ISBN: 978-0-367-02913-5 (hbk)
ISBN: 978-0-367-02915-9 (pbk)
ISBN: 978-0-429-00121-5 (ebk)

Typeset in Baskerville
by Newgen Publishing UK

For Clarence

Contents

Acknowledgments   x

Introduction   1

1 Fast-Track to Deep Waters: Why Work with Dreams?   8
A Matter of Life and Death 9
A Brief Summary of Research into Clinical Usefulness of Dreams 10
Why Work with Dreams? 12

2 Bringing It Home: Inviting Dreamwork into Your Practice, and Your Life   19
Reasons for Therapists to Attend to Our Dreams 20
Recalling and Recording Dreams 21
Working with Dreams, Both in and out of Therapy 22
The "Silent Epidemic" of Sleep and Dream Deprivation 23
Beyond Sleep Deprivation to REM/Dream Loss 24
One Way to Work with Your Own Dreams: Bias Control 26

3 Common Factors: Toward a Universal Approach to Working with Dreams   27
Mapping Common Pathways of Dreamwork 28
Common Factors in Context 29
A Clear Trend toward Experiential Methods 30
A Proposed Generic Dreamwork Method Based on Common Factors 31
Defining the Steps 32
Optional Avenues 34

4 Mapping the Route: The Science of Dreaming   38
Dreaming as Another Form of Thought 39
What Is the Function of a Dream? 40
Theories of Dream Function: Competing or Complementary? 41
Dreams as "Memory Consolidation in Action" 43

viii Contents

5 Understanding the Terrain: The Dream Is Born in Metaphor 49
   The Physical Basis of Metaphor 49
   Metaphor as a Vehicle for Emergent Meaning 51
   Bear in the Kitchen Dream 52
   The Underwater Woman 53
   Runaway Jeep Dream 54

6 From Ordinary to Sublime: Kinds of Dreams 58
   Big Dreams 59
   Impactful Dreams 60
   Lucid Dreams 61
   Kinds of Disturbing Dreams: Nightmares, Night Terrors and Sleep Paralysis 62
   Precognitive Dreams 63
   Recurrent Dreams and Dream Series 63

7 Navigating the Dream Divide: Woman in the Mirror Dream 66
   The "Dream Divide" 67
   The Divide as a Function of Our Bilateral Brain 68
   Expanding Perspectives: More Ways to Consider Dreams 69
   The Dreamwork Decision Tree 70
   Woman in the Mirror Dream 71
   Finding a Good Stopping Place 76

8 The Central Quest: Finding the Life Force Inherent in All Dreams 79
   Forms of Help and How to Find It 80
   Gabby and the "Holy Trinity" 81
   Entering the Dream 83
   The Following Sessions 83
   Help Can Come from Unlikely Places 85

9 Avenues of Exploration: Visual Art and Technology 87
   Working with Art and Images 88
   Dreamwork as Performance Art 89
   Visualizing Dreams: What the Future Holds 93

10 The Inner Journey: Dreams and the Body 95
   Experiencing the Dream from the Inside 96
   Jungian Approaches to Body Dreamwork 97
   A Focusing Approach to Dreamwork 99
   The Dream of the Perfect Newborn 100

11 Perfect Storms: Working with Nightmares and Bad Dreams 103
   De-Escalating the Fear 104
   Grateful Dead Dream Session 104
   Finding Help as a Form of Resourcing 108

Working with PTSD Nightmares 109
Exposure and Mastery: Proposed Mechanisms of Action 110

12 Fellow Travelers: Working with Dreams in Groups 112
Taylor's Projective Dreamwork 113
The Lion Dream Session: An Ullman Group Process 114
The Dreamer's Reflections 119

13 How Dreams Enlarge Us: Big Dreams 121
The Honoré Women Dream Session 122
Observations and Commentary 130
Dreams as Preparation for Death: Facing the Sabretooth 130

14 Transformation: Applying Neuroscience to Dreamwork 132
Dreams and an Updated Definition of the Unconscious 133
Emotional Memory Reconsolidation: A Cause for Optimism 135
Doing What Dreams Do, Only Better 136
Dreamwork as More Art than Science 139
Clinical Examples of Transformational Dreamwork 140
The "new was" 141
Summary of Lessons from This Book: Why and How to Work with Dreams 141
In Closing 142
Embryo in the Water Dream 143

Index 145

Acknowledgments

There are so many people I would like to acknowledge and thank for their support and encouragement throughout the research and writing of this book. First, thanks to my family, especially Jim and Grace, for your ongoing encouragement and willingness to engage in so many conversations about dreams. And thanks to my sister Leah for her whimsical sketches.

I truly appreciate all of the people who offered to read various drafts and offer your expertise, feedback and suggestions. Thank you to Jane Makin, David Ceilak, David Jenkins, Chris Edwards, Jan Winhall and Mark Blagrove. Also thanks to Mark Blagrove, Stan Krippner and Jacquie Lewis for your review and support of my initial proposal. Thanks to Bill O'Hanlon for helping me get the ball rolling on this project and to Robert Bosnak for kick-starting my creativity.

Many people also contributed personal or clinical material, engaged in helpful conversations about specific aspects of this book, and/or engaged in dream groups and dreamwork sessions. In this regard, I especially want to thank Sue Cornfield and Gabby, David Jenkins, Josie Malinowski, Michelle Carr, Chris Edwards, Kitt Price, Shaila Patel, Priscilla Coleff, Karen Coulombe, Dean Diamond, Emily Batchelder, George Hanson, Robbyn Peters-Bennett, Charlotte Underwood, Jen Levin and Ilaria Franchi.

For confidentiality reasons, there are many more of you who I will not name, but I am grateful to as well: thanks to *all* my dreamwork groups, clients, students, colleagues, friends, family … every one of you who generously shared your dreams and allowed me to use examples of your dreamwork practice for this book. You and your dreams are what make the material come to life, and you have all taught me so much.

Introduction

In your work as a therapist, do you sometimes feel stymied and wish for creative inspiration to deepen the therapy process and help clients who are stuck move forward? Dreams are like a wise and trusted supervisor who reliably points you toward the emotional truth and the most salient aspects of your client's current life situation. And occasionally dreams go beyond this steady guidance and bring images of stunning depth and creativity that lead to insight, healing, and a call to action. If taken seriously, these "big" dreams can lead to transformation. The beauty of dreams is that the information they bring comes directly from the dreamer, unfiltered and unhampered by the internal censor that operates during waking hours. Dreams unearth deep truths that may be hard, even impossible, to reach otherwise, and they are not distorted by either the client's blind spots or by your own; they simply tell it like it is.

Despite their often bizarre and ethereal qualities, dreams can be a rich source of meaning and insight. Yet the clinical use of dreams has become limited, sporadic and most often initiated by clients, not clinicians. This book is intended to de-mystify and encourage the use of dream work in clinical practice by providing a road map to doing dream work with clarity and confidence. It draws from the most effective approaches to the dream, those that have not only stood the test of time but also are practical, understandable and generally agreed-upon by dream workers in clinical practice today. You will also be guided through a process of discovery of what's relevant to you as a therapist from the vast world of dream research. In short, this book will provide you with our current and best understanding of what dreams are and how to work with them. It will also give you a simple road map to guide you in the process of working with your clients' dreams. The process is easier to facilitate than you may think because your client is the only true expert on their dreams, and you are there simply as a guide and companion. Curiosity and caring, plus a few simple ideas or tracks to follow are sufficient for you to engage in effective dream work. Too often, therapists avoid dreamwork because they feel they need to be able to figure the dream out, but this is actually a collaborative process that depends mostly on the client, and what comes to them when they spend time experiencing and exploring their dream. As the therapist, *you already have the tools* to help them do this: empathy, curiosity and the deep listening skills you have developed as part of your job.

2 *Introduction*

One of the essential pieces of knowledge that helps us and our clients to benefit from the unique form of consciousness that dreams are is a basic understanding of the dream's manner of communicating. Despite what Freud wrote about the subject, modern dream workers tend to believe that dreams do not deliberately distort their messages but instead are as clear and straightforward as it is possible for them to be given the particular constraints of dream consciousness. Once these constraints and some of the mechanisms that create our dreams are generally understood, dream messages are much easier to explore and decipher. The steps to do so will be provided later in this book so you can immediately begin using the methods described, as appropriate to your own way of working. I am hoping the book will inspire you to have much more frequent and fruitful conversations about dreams in your therapy room.

If dreams are such a valuable therapeutic ally, why has the psychotherapy profession moved so far away from its dream-centric roots? Far from being standard practice, the use of dreams is now rarely taught to new clinicians unless they are specifically pursuing a modality, such as psychoanalysis, Jungian or depth psychotherapy, where dream work remains central. In the general push toward evidence-based practices, goal-oriented, clearly-mapped and time-limited courses of therapy, dreams have lost their central place. I strongly believe that as therapists, this is to our detriment. There is increasing new or confirming evidence to support the value and efficacy of dream work. There is also a large body of scientific knowledge about dreams that has been percolating for decades but that has not been effectively integrated into clinical practice. There is a relationship between clinical dream work and the emerging field of interpersonal neurobiology that has barely been touched upon because some of the ideas are so current there has not been time for them to integrate into the ever-evolving practice of psychotherapy. And finally, there are new ways of working with dreams based on specific methods that have a solid evidence base, that are indispensable for specific applications. For example, imagery rehearsal therapy (IRT) has been shown to significantly reduce nightmare frequency and distress in those who suffer from PTSD-related nightmares. And the mechanics of emotional memory reconsolidation delineate the accessible and specific steps that can lead to emotional transformation using dream work.

In the field of psychotherapy in general, there is mounting support for approaches that access implicit information and life experience not accessible through the more direct channels of conscious, cognitive inquiry. Many of the issues clients bring to therapy have their roots in early relational patterns and embodied memories that were never made explicit. As such, these deep emotional patterns cannot be talked about in the usual way that one might discuss "presenting issues" and ideas about their origins and solutions. Some of our deepest concerns do not have words, and these are the very areas to which dreams can direct our attention. Dreams also offer new information, and thus can point the way toward healing and constructive change.

It is most often lack of training and knowledge that prevents therapists from working with dreams, and this fuels the perception that dream work has to be time-consuming and complex. However, dream work has changed since the days of Freud and Jung, and is now much more collaborative, creative and highly

Introduction 3

engaging for both therapists and clients. The dream research community has discovered much about the process of dreaming that can be applied in therapy, so dreams are not as mysterious as they once were. Research into dreaming is beginning to establish some plausible theories about the purpose of dreams; this development is relatively new and continually evolving. Current research has validated some dream work practices, and debunked others, but the worlds of psychotherapy and dream research do not cross-pollinate enough. One of the aims of this book is to bridge the two domains wherever possible, and to bring clinicians up to speed on the science and theory that is most relevant to working with dreams in today's practice.

The current scientific theories that have the most support suggest that dreams facilitate the consolidation of memory and/or the process of emotional regulation. Both activities are also key functions of psychotherapy so it makes sense to weave them together in a way that brings combined benefits that are greater than the sum of their parts. Many dream researchers suggest dreaming does its therapeutic work whether we spend time with our dreams or not. But even those who think dream content itself may be a random byproduct of the sleeping brain also believe that spending time with dream material is beneficial, simply not to be confused with the impact (or lack thereof) of dreaming itself.

It *is* important to differentiate what dreams themselves do and what therapists can do *with* them. There is considerable clinical evidence, and some empirical data to support the notion that dream work is experienced by psychotherapy clients as meaningful and therapeutic. But given the voluminous and sometimes contradictory nature of the literature on dreams and the mysterious nature of dreams themselves, many clinicians view dream work as daunting. This book is intended to offer clarity, justification and a path for clinicians to entertain the illuminating and creative dream worlds of our clients as a way to help them move forward, gain insight, and work through their deepest concerns. There are simple, tried-and-true methods to navigate any dream and this book provides a clear road map that synthesizes the best of the current approaches.

Fast-Track to Deep Waters: Why Work with Dreams?

Chapter 1 spells out the benefits of incorporating dream work into clinical practice and is sprinkled with salient examples. In addition to turning our attention to deeper matters, the benefits of working with dreams include the fact that dreams are creative and engage clients in the therapy process. They point to our most salient emotional concerns. They bypass our internal editing process and normal defenses, and so are unflinchingly honest representations of our life situation. Dreams can bring a new and wider perspective on a situation that seems stuck. They provide diagnostic information and can be an indicator of clinical progress. They help to regulate our emotions, and working directly with the feelings dreams engender may strengthen this positive effect. They can be a safe pathway to working with trauma. The "big" dreams we occasionally experience can literally change our lives, and dream therapy can facilitate and integrate this transformation. Each of these points is expanded upon and explained, followed by a brief summary of research into the clinical use of dreams. Taken as a whole, the first chapter is intended to bring new information and appreciation for dream work, and a sense of confidence that such a thing is accessible and useful to all therapists, regardless of theoretical orientation.

Bringing It Home: Inviting Dreamwork into Your Practice, and Your Life

Chapter 2 covers the basics of where to begin if you want to support your clients to bring dreams to their sessions. Many of these same techniques can be used to explore your own dreams, a practice that is invaluable for learning the language of dreamwork. Working with your dreams on your own, or better yet with a group, partner or therapist, is the best way to learn dreamwork and to develop a genuine appreciation for the depth and ingenuity of dreams. What follows is practical information for anyone with an interest in working with their dreams, including how to recall and record them, and something even more basic as a prerequisite to dreaming: getting a good nights' sleep! The current sleep and dream deprivation crisis is explored, along with potential solutions.

Common Factors: Toward a Universal Dreamwork Method

As a first step in writing this book, I conducted a study of my own to determine the common factors in current dreamwork practices. Chapter 3 provides the result of my qualitative inquiry, which concluded that there is a distinct trend away from interpretation and toward experiential approaches to the dream. The chapter provides a list of all the most common dreamwork techniques in use today, as well as a brief explanation of each. Using these tried-and-true techniques, I sketch out a universal approach to working with dreams that allows enough flexibility for therapists to adapt it to their own theoretical orientation.

Mapping the Route: The Science of Dreaming

Academic dream research is a world apart from the type of inquiry into dreams that takes place in a therapist's office. Despite this, I would argue that it is useful to have some knowledge of the assumptions we are making when we work with our clients' dreams, and also to know something about the field of dream research because this body of work can shape, guide and update our interventions. Chapter 4 covers a select history of dream research, including a summary of the major current theories about the function(s) of dreaming. The research into dreaming is voluminous, complex and at times, contradictory. I have simplified and pared it down to the most clinically-relevant material.

Understanding the Terrain: A Dream Is Born in Metaphor

Dreams do more than simply speak the language of metaphor, many would suggest that they *are* metaphor. Understanding the dreamscape as expressed in metaphor helps us make sense of it, and to see that a dream is not the mind's attempt to obscure, but rather the body's attempt to communicate in the way that comes most naturally. Much of the strangeness and apparent obscurity of dreams is removed as soon as we understand that we should not always take them literally but rather view them metaphorically as well. Chapter 5 describes metaphor as a fundamental way we understand and communicate rather than as merely a linguistic device. It presents some dream examples and how one might view them as metaphors for aspects of the dreamer's life.

From Ordinary to Sublime: Kinds of Dreams

A critical factor in deciding which is the best way to work with someone's dream is the *type* of dream they bring. You would work very differently with a harrowing nightmare than you would with an uplifting spiritual dream. Throughout history, there have been many systems developed to categorize dreams, many that pre-date the clinical use of dreams. The debate about the nature of dreams continues to this day. In Chapter 6, some of the most prevalent systems and specific kinds of dreams are presented, as well as considerations about how to work with the various types of dreams.

Navigating the Dream Divide: Woman in the Mirror Dream

There is a distinct trend in modern dreamwork toward greater experiential exploration of dreams and away from interpretation. However, there remains a philosophical divide about the essential direction and purpose of dreamwork, which reflects polarized beliefs about the nature of dreams. Some dreamworkers make the connection of dreams to waking life situations central to their method, while others suggest we avoid this at all costs in favor of an interactive experience with the dream itself. Chapter 7 first offers an explanation of the "dream divide" in terms of neuroscience, and then uses some selections from the menu of "common factors" choices to provide a detailed example of the avenues used in a focusing-oriented dreamwork session, which falls on the dream-centric (vs. self-centric) side of the dream divide.

The Central Quest: Finding the Life Force Inherent in Dreams

Gendlin believed that every dream brings some form of 'help' that contains within it the energy to propel the dreamer's life forward. After 20 years of working with dreams, I have come to believe this as well. Finding and aligning with the helpful forces in a dream allows the dreamer to feel more secure, more resourced, more able to move forward into the challenging terrain that may lie ahead. Chapter 8 offers clinical examples, including a case study that covers the client's progress over many sessions and illustrates the process and the value of finding 'help' in dreams.

Avenues of Exploration: Visual Art and Technology

In Chapter 9, I offer examples of working with a dream visually. Dreams most often come to us in the form of images, sometimes incredibly rich in detail and complexity. When we wake up we usually try to capture our dreams by making a story out of them. However, this human tendency to form a narrative to make sense of our experience does not always do justice to the dream, and sometimes truly alters it. Visual art speaks a language that is closer to dreaming, so it is often helpful to ask our clients to depict their dreams by sketching or painting them, and in the process, new information and insight often emerges. The chapter ends with a look at dream depiction of the future.

The Inner Journey: Dreams and the Body

Chapter 10 describes a personal journey to a small Mexican town where I participated in a week-long embodied imagination workshop with Robert Bosnak. I compare and integrate this method with my own modality, that of focusing-oriented dreamwork. I describe the arc of the dream journey and how it shifted my perspective away from connecting my dream life to my waking life, and more toward the dreaming as an experience unto itself. This dialectic is a theme that runs throughout this book.

Perfect Storms: Working with Nightmares and Bad Dreams

Nightmares are among the most dramatic kinds of dreams, and can be both the most frightening and the most transformative. There is considerable recent research demonstrating that rescripting the ending of dreams is an effective treatment for those whose disturbed dreaming has become a serious problem, and/or is part of the symptomology of PTSD. Chapter 11 describes the research, as well as my own study using dreamwork to treat the nightmares of refugees. A clinical example of how one might dream the dream onward as a way to work with a nightmare is included, as well as a follow-up conversation with the dreamer who explained how the work dissipated the dream's emotional charge.

Fellow Travelers: Working with Dreams in Groups

Two of the most prevalent ways to work with dreams in groups were developed by Montague Ullman and Jeremy Taylor, and both are transparent in their use of projections by group members as a key part of the dreamwork process. Group process with dreams is a wonderful way to demonstrate the incredible depth and richness that can come from a dream. The process also teaches members exactly how it feels to project one's own material onto someone else's dream. In Chapter 12, group dreamwork is briefly introduced, and a clinical example follows that illustrates the power of the process.

How Dreams Enlarge Us: Big Dreams

Jung coined the term "big dreams" to characterize those dreams that come with a clear, often spiritual message that has an immediate impact that may continue throughout the dreamer's life. In Chapter 13, an extended clinical example illustrates one way of exploring a big dream, and also shows how these dreams are qualitatively quite different from our more frequent and typical dreams. The featured dream takes the dreamer on an epic journey that confirms her longing for time alone to pursue the depths of her spiritual life.

Transformation: Applying Neuroscience to Dreamwork

Chapter 14 proposes a model of dreamwork guided by our current understanding of the neurobiology of both dreaming and of transformational change. I begin by summarizing an updated view of the unconscious and dreaming in light of current neuroscience. I then offer a very brief and selective synthesis of how dreams may contribute to memory reconsolidation, how memory reconsolidation facilitates transformation, and how these two phenomena might work together in a clinical setting. I suggest that dreams can provide an important avenue for therapists to facilitate emotional memory reconsolidation. Because there has been considerable advancement in our knowledge of these processes over the past decade or two, it is now possible to understand more about how new learning and change happen during the various stages of sleep, giving us a more sure-footed approach to transformational dreamwork. The chapter will include a clinical example to ground these ideas in practice. I conclude with an overview of the terrain covered in this book and an optimistic sense of the future of dreamwork.

A Note on Dream Examples

I am extremely grateful to all the clients, students and practitioners who offered their dreams and examples of their dreamwork to help illustrate the concepts presented here. I used client dreams sparingly and only with their express permission, and with identifying information altered. I have presented several personal examples because I feel more comfortable commenting on and dissecting my own dreams versus subjecting the dreams of others to such treatment. Students in my dream groups and classes were also very generous with permission to use the transcripts of our dreamwork to provide readers with a sense of what actually happens in session, providing a clearer sense of how to put theory into practice. *Thank you* to all of you who shared your dreams!

1 Fast-Track to Deep Waters
Why Work with Dreams?

Illustrations by Leah Lyon

> *Dreams are the touchstones of our characters.*
>
> Henry David Thoreau

Why should therapists in clinical practice have a practical understanding of how to work with clients' dreams? There are many good reasons, now more well-understood than ever, that dreamwork can deepen and accelerate the process of therapy. Dream researchers have been working for decades amassing evidence that supports the notion that dreams are relevant and helpful to us in many specific ways. But the worlds of dream research and dream therapy rarely overlap, though each could inform and enrich the other. Many clinicians and clinical training programs reject dreamwork as too esoteric or antiquated for modern psychotherapy, but I would argue that an appreciation of the science of dreaming may help to restore dreamwork to its rightful place as an essential aspect of psychotherapy, and a critical part of any therapist's skill set.

I will begin with a personal example which demonstrates how dreams can facilitate more efficient therapy by bringing the conversation right to the heart of matters that concern us most deeply. This story will show how dreams can reach far back into our personal history and weave together experiences that have important features in common. Such dreams can be a way to help us manage and integrate the intense feelings associated with the events they portray. Hartmann (2001) believes dreams are like therapy because both activities involve "making connections in a safe place." The following example illustrates how the beneficial effects of dreams and psychotherapy can be combined for an even more powerful effect than each would have on their own.

A Matter of Life and Death

The subject of this clinical example is literally a matter of life and death. I've had more than one close encounter with death, and the first was very early in life. I was born two months premature, weighing just three pounds, and although survival rates for preemies have improved dramatically since the mid-60s, back then I was not expected to survive. In fact, of the four preemies born in that cold midwinter week in Saskatchewan, I was the only one that did not die. While I have no explicit memories of those first precarious days, I know that at the time, there was no understanding of the physical holding and comfort every newborn needs to thrive. Instead, we were kept in pristine incubators and touched only as needed to meet our basic needs because germs were considered the biggest threat to survival. It was two months before I was deemed healthy enough to go home, so my start in life was marked by minimal physical contact and a deep sense of aloneness.

I had another near-death experience 17 years later. Feeling all the invincibility of an adolescent, I attempted to dive under a waterfall into a glacial mountain river. I got caught in a strong current that pulled me deep under the surface. Many years later, I had a vivid dream that blended images of both of these experiences. I was in a clear glass box that was caught in the whirlpool of a river, and when I reached out for help, no one was there. The dream brought intense feelings and sensations of that day on the river back to life and it put me in direct contact with a deep, familiar sense of aloneness that I had known all my life. I was in therapy at the time with a Jungian analyst, sorting through my personal history, informing my own work as a therapist and amassing the hours I needed so I might train to become an analyst myself. Naturally I told the dream to my analyst, and as is often suggested in Jungian therapy, drew images of the dream, and spent time in direct experiential contact with the powerful feelings it evoked. In one unforgettable session, we enacted the dream, and when I reached out for help, he took a firm grasp of my hand and met me there, reaching across the years and letting that newborn part of me feel his clear and solid contact. It was so unexpected it sent a shock wave through my body. The work we did with that dream was probably the most profound of any therapy I have done. Yet if I had not had the dream, I think I might have stayed with more everyday subject matter such as my relationship concerns and the personal decisions I was contemplating. This dream took me into much deeper, more meaningful terrain and was a catalyst for change at an implicit level that is difficult to describe. Some tangible changes were that I deepened many of my relationships and became less of a lone wolf, much more readily able to recruit support and company in personal and professional endeavors. Some impactful dreams bring about changes like this all by themselves, but sometimes, as in this case, the dream was the catalyst, but *the change took place in the context of therapy*. I would suggest that even if the dream itself is transformational, working with it in therapy provides a venue for integration of the insights and concrete realization of the changes the dream has the potential to engender. Dreams unfold in the telling, and can stay relevant and alive, and at various stages in our lives can reveal additional facets of meaning.

Clinicians who do not pay attention to their clients' dreams are missing an opportunity to add a compelling dimension of depth, meaning and emotional authenticity to the therapy process. Because dreams often speak the language of metaphor, even the most seemingly mundane content may carry important meaning that is outside of the dreamer's immediate awareness. For example, a client who regularly brings dreams to therapy told me in one session that she had lots of dreams the previous night, but nothing important. Her dogs were in the dream, doing what they always do: the younger one pestering the older one who was, in the dream, getting to the point where she simply couldn't take it anymore and was ready to snap. While acknowledging the dream snippet was literally true, the simple query, "Is there anything in your life like that, anything that you are completely fed up with?" opened up a whole avenue of process around her situation at work that was aptly represented by the dogs. It also turned out to be a huge relief to discuss a topic that may well have been left unexplored had she not mentioned her dream.

In addition to turning our attention to deeper matters, the benefits of working with dreams in clinical practice include the fact that dreams are creative and engage clients in the therapy process. They point to our most salient emotional concerns. They bypass our internal editing process and normal defenses, and so are unflinchingly honest representations of our life situation. Dreams can bring a new and wider perspective on a situation that seems otherwise stuck. They provide diagnostic information and can be indicators of clinical progress. They help to regulate our emotions, and working directly with the feelings dreams engender may strengthen this positive effect. They can be a safe pathway to working with trauma. The "big" dreams we occasionally experience can literally change our lives, and dream therapy can facilitate and integrate this transformation. (Each of these benefits will be discussed more fully later in the chapter.)

A Brief Summary of Research into Clinical Usefulness of Dreams

Much of what we know about how clinicians use dreams in their practice is captured in a handful of studies that were reviewed by Pesant and Zadra (2004) with the goal of making clinicians aware that integrating dreamwork into their practice is both beneficial and accessible. The researchers found that while most therapists do work with dreams at least occasionally in their practice, the majority are not comfortable doing so because they feel they lack expertise or the necessary specialized training. In fact, it is most often the clients, not the therapists, who initiate dreamwork. The review also found evidence that dreamwork helps increase clients' self-knowledge and insight, and increases their commitment to therapy, which can be a predictor of good therapy outcomes. The researchers concluded that "there is strong evidence that clinicians have much to gain by attending to their clients' dreams, and that effective dream work is accessible to most clinicians."

A year later, Eudell-Simmons and Hilsenroth (2005) reviewed the clinical literature on dreamwork with a focus on four areas: therapeutic process, client insight and self-awareness, dreams as a source of information for the therapist and dreams as a measure of therapeutic change. The latter two categories have received less attention than the former. The authors found evidence that dreams are an excellent source of client information, especially of details the client is otherwise unable or unwilling to reveal. They also found evidence that changes in dreams can indicate progress in therapy, and overall that dreamwork is at least as effective a form of therapy as other approaches.

There is some evidence that there may be particular benefit to discussion of dreams (Edwards et. al., 2015). A study of dream group experiences compared discussion of a significant life event versus a discussion of dreams and found participants perceived significantly higher insight gains as a result of discussing their dreams. The study was with a non-clinical sample and the insight gains were achieved using the Ullman group method. Edwards noted the importance of distinguishing true personal insight from the "aha" of recognition the dreamer has from merely identifying the memory source of the dream. Many times I have seen people dismiss their dreams once they recognize the actual life experience that the dream was drawn from, as if that explains it away. But in my experience, it's better to think of life events as the palette from which the dream draws its material, though the final work of art may represent something else entirely.

The majority of research into the effectiveness of dreamwork in a clinical setting has been led by Clara Hill, and taken as a whole, the results supporting the use of dreams in therapy are convincing. More than 25 studies are summarized in two reviews (Hill & Goates, 2004; Hill & Knox, 2010) and all were conducted using the dreamwork method Hill developed, the cognitive-experiential dream model. The method begins with an experiential exploration of the dream, followed by a stage where the client offers insights into the dream's meaning gained from the experiential phase, and finally, there is an action step where client and therapist discuss changes the client might make as a result of the dreamwork.

One finding that emerged from Hill's studies is that clients clearly enjoy working with their dreams; in 12 separate studies, clients consistently rated the quality of the dreamwork sessions as significantly higher than the quality of their regular therapy sessions. Clients also consistently reported gaining greater insight into their dreams after dreamwork sessions, and this insight increased in the two weeks following the session. Before the dream therapy, clients generally reported poor understanding of their dreams, suggesting that working with dreams in therapy brings benefits from dreams that would otherwise not be realized. Spangler and Hill (2015) summarized the results of the research noting that positive change in outcomes related to dreams was clear, with significant improvement in session quality, attitude toward dreams, insight, ideas for ways to take action and specific problem solving. More general outcomes were mixed, although some of the research showed a decrease in depression and an increase in well-being after dreamwork, as well as higher self-esteem and greater insight for those engaged in dream groups compared to waitlist controls.

The other area where there is clear evidence of the efficacy of working with dreams is in the area of treating PTSD nightmares. Imagery Rehearsal Therapy (Krakow et al. 2000, 2001) has been shown in several large clinical trials to significantly reduce PTSD symptoms. Lucid dreaming as a nightmare treatment method is also gaining empirical support (Spoormaker & van den Bout, 2006). These and other ways to treat nightmares using dreamwork will be discussed in the chapter on nightmares.

More recently, Leonard and Dawson (2018) mapped out the historical and cultural reasons dreamwork has been marginalized in psychotherapy, and they strongly advocate for change. The authors point to many important reasons to include dreamwork in clinical practice (all of which are covered in this chapter). They also warn of the potential loss of rapport with the client and the sense clients will have that the therapist is not interested in their inner life if they do not engage with their dreams. The authors conclude that change is needed, and should begin with telling a more complete story about the state of modern dreamwork:

> The dominant discourse of dreams having no psychological meaning or clinical value is only one side of the story in a short chapter within humanity's long history of fascination with dreams. In our view, the theoretical diversity in dream theory offers multiple pathways for contemporary psychologists to engage in dream work in ways that are achievable within the constraints of contemporary practice, including time limits and preferences for particular theoretical orientations.
>
> (Leonard and Dawson, 2018)

Why Work with Dreams?

They Are Creative and Engage Our Clients in the Therapy Process

Dreams are novel and fascinating products of our imagination and consciousness and as such are inherently interesting. Everybody dreams and has had the experience of waking up terrified, excited or deeply moved by the drama that just unfolded in their mind while they were sleeping. Although the process of therapy can be challenging, one of the things that keeps clients engaged is the incredible gift of being listened to deeply and respectfully. We are human; we all love to be seen and appreciated, and sharing our dreams with an interested, curious listener is compelling and engaging. As a therapist, you will engage your clients more deeply, and also help them step outside of their habitual dialogue when you pay attention to their dreams.

They Point to Our Most Salient Emotional Concerns

It may seem that we don't need dreams to do this, but that we are always well aware of our most pressing emotional concerns. However, human consciousness is not always straightforward or consistent, and people can be very good at unwittingly deceiving themselves. In fact, one of the most popular forms of therapy (cognitive-behavioral therapy, or CBT) was founded on the premise that our mind leads us astray and distorts our experience in a number of ways. One example is rationalization, a habit of talking ourselves out of our feelings using "rational" arguments, such as, "I'm not sad that she left; I didn't really love her anyway." We can often fool our conscious mind, but such a person may dream of losing something of great value and wake up crying. If they pay attention to their dream, they will realize that they are in fact very sad about the loss of their relationship. Dreams are like that very good friend who is willing to be honest with us even when what they have to say is not easy to hear.

Dreams can also provide therapy clients with a way to introduce important yet deeply personal topics in the course of therapy, subjects they may want to bring up but are reluctant to do so due to fear, embarrassment or cultural norms that discourage personal revelation, even in therapy (Tien, Lin & Chen, 2006). Goelitz (2007), who works with clients preparing for death, found that dreamwork brought the focus of the session to the deeper emotional concerns rather than the more typical discussions about physical symptoms and treatment. She noted that the dreamwork helped her clients feel less alone and better prepared for death. She was convinced that these discussions would not have taken place had they not been facilitated by a dream.

Dreams Bypass Our Internal Editing Process and Normal Defenses and So Are Honest Representations of Our Life Situation

Dreams tell the truth, even when such truth is uncomfortable and defended against in everyday awareness. During sleep our prefrontal cortices, responsible for, among other things, rational thought and executive functioning, mostly shut down for the night. During dreaming, our internal editor, and our moral authority also go to sleep. That's why our dreams can sometimes be bizarre and why normally taboo subject matter such as explicit sexuality and violence can often appear in our dreams. At times, it seems as though our dreaming consciousness is trying to get our attention by delivering its content in the most flamboyant or dramatic way possible. It helps to know that dreams are often metaphorical, not meant to be taken literally. For example, I had a dream that I was eating horseshit and kind of enjoying it even though I was well aware of how disgusting this would seem to the people around me. I laughed to myself when I understood the dream's message might have to do with a lecture I had listened to a few days' prior that I found highly entertaining and yet filled with ideas I considered completely far-fetched. Because I liked the person, I was trying to remain open to their ideas, trying to take in and digest the material, but having trouble doing so. The dream captured the complexity of my feeling about the situation with economy and humor.

There is considerable clinical evidence to suggest that dreams carry emotional truth that is often difficult for the dreamer to assimilate (Ecker & Hulley, 1996). One of the major benefits I have seen in working with dreams is that it can help clients to see and truly experience an unconscious aspect of their personality or behavior that is not congruent with how they see themselves or want to be (Ellis, 2013). For example, a client I will call Michael had a dream that he was walking on a beach and came across a group of people sitting in a circle, and his cousin was there with them smoking a crack pipe. Michael had a strong judgement about this, as smoking crack was something he would never do. But if, as some theories suggest, characters in a dream represent aspects of ourselves, then Michael was like his dream-cousin in some way. In the dreamwork he did, I asked him to "be" his cousin on the beach, and when he imagined this, he felt an attraction to the pipe, and then a dawning of awareness that this feeling of addiction was familiar to him as it colored the dynamic of his relationships with the women in his life. He was flooded with shame and a heartfelt desire to change which fueled transformation in his relationship and many other aspects of his life.

Dreams Can Bring a New and Wider Perspective on a Situation that Is Stuck or Static

History provides many good examples of how a dream can bring a creative new perspective. The person who invented and patented the first lock-stitch sewing machine solved the main challenges to developing a reliable machine because a dream pointed to the solution that had long eluded him. Elias Howe, who eventually became the second-wealthiest man in the United States, came up with the novel idea of putting the hole in the "wrong" end of the needle from a dream of a spear fight between warring native tribes. In the dream, some of the warriors' spears punctured the fabric of the tents, snagged loops of thread and pulled them back through with the tips of their spears. Dreams are the sources of many great inventions, including the periodic table and Einstein's theory of relativity. For someone who has studied a subject deeply but who has become stuck in a fixed way of looking at the problem, dreams can bring the fresh creative inspiration that was elusive. Sometimes "sleeping on it" can bring unexpected and creative answers. For a thorough treatment of dream creativity, see Barrett (2001).

Dreams are embodied, and present us with an internally generated world that is detailed and appears very real to all of our senses. This total immersion brings us in touch with the magical quality of dreaming. A dream is a richly detailed world that is experienced as entirely real while the person is dreaming it. Even for those who experience lucid dreaming and become aware they are dreaming while in the midst of it, the experience feels very real. This aspect of dreams is what makes them so compelling, and such a useful tool in therapy for assisting clients in stepping out of their ordinary way of experiencing or seeing things. A dream can bring a broader perspective, a new way of seeing, a shift from ordinary consciousness, or habitual ideas, a step toward change.

Dreams Provide Diagnostic Information and Can Be Indicators of Clinical Progress

There are many ways that dreams can provide diagnostic information about clients, although the subject is a complex one because dreams can be cryptic. According to Sacks (1996) dreams are, "directly or distortedly, reflections of current states of body and mind." Neurological disorders can alter dreaming processes in quite specific ways, and these can vary from person to person. Sacks gives the example of a patient with an occipital angioma who knew that if his dreams turned from their usual black and white to red, he was about to have a seizure. Some other examples Sacks offered are loss of visual imagery in dreams as a possible precursor to Alzheimer's, and recovery dreams presaging remission from multiple sclerosis. Sacks hypothesized that the dreaming mind is more sensitive than the waking mind to subtle changes in the body, and so appears prescient because it picks up subtle early cues.

In some cases, this premonitory aspect of dreaming can even be life-saving. Taylor (1992) offered the example of a woman from a dream group that met regularly who dreamt of a purse of rotting meat. The dream was so disturbing to her and the other group members, the woman felt unsettled enough to have a diagnostic pap smear which turned out to be negative. She insisted on further testing which revealed she had a particularly aggressive form of uterine cancer that would have killed her had she not caught it in time. At the time of the dream she had no symptoms and was about to go on a trip – she credits the dream and the dreamwork for saving her life.

Not only can dreams be indicative of potential health changes for better or worse, they can also be used to track clinical progress. Tracking shifts or progress via dreams can be an easier task for therapists than using a dream to make an initial diagnosis because it is often easier to spot incremental change in the pattern of dreaming than to decipher something completely new. It takes some time to get to know the unique world of each dreamer, and paying attention to a series of dreams will make it clearer when something significant has changed. For example, in my research into the nature and treatment of recurrent PTSD nightmares (Ellis, 2016), specific kinds of changes in dreams that had been recurring repeatedly, sometimes for years, appeared to coincide with trauma recovery. This observation is supported by research that sampled 94 trauma survivors and found the closer their nightmares were to replicating the actual trauma event, the higher their level of related distress (Davis, Byrd, Rhudy & Wright, 2007). For trauma therapists who track dreams, the progression from concrete to less realistic, more imaginative dreaming can be seen as a sign of clinical progress.

Dreams Help to Regulate Our Emotions, and Working Directly with the Feelings Dreams Engender May Strengthen This Positive Effect

The notion that dreams help regulate emotion is not a new one. Freud (1900/2010) suggested that the function of dreaming was to preserve sleep by attenuating emotional distress. Many dream theorists and researchers have built and expanded upon this hypothesis and amassed a convincing body of evidence to support the notion. For example, Kramer (1991) was able to show that dreams, and not simply sleep, are responsible for consistent improvement in mood from evening to morning. The exception to this is when the dreamer has a nightmare, which Kramer saw as a failure in dream function. Kramer proposed a mood regulatory function of dreaming, suggesting "the 'emotional surge' that accompanies rapid-eye movement (REM) sleep is contained by the psychological experience of dreaming. The nightmare occurs when the integrative capacity of the dreamer is exceeded." He saw dreams as a kind of "emotional thermostat."

In addition to emotional regulation, another well-supported theory is that dreams are involved in the consolidation of memories. In dreaming we appear to be sorting through the countless impressions and events of the day and determining which become preserved in long-term memory. We forget the vast majority of what we take in, and need a way to separate what is valuable enough to retain explicitly from what is not. A key factor in determining what we remember and what we forget is its emotional intensity. This is common sense: we remember what deeply affects us. Given the strength of theories that implicate dreams in both emotional regulation and memory consolidation, it is reasonable to suggest that dreams perform a kind of sorting process, laying down important events in the associative networks that make up our memories, and privileging those new experiences that made a distinct impression upon us. This is why dreams can be such valuable tools for therapy. They point to what matters to us.

Dreams Can Be a Safe Pathway to Working with Trauma

Traumatic life events and their sequelae are often what bring people into therapy. Clients generally don't want to work through the traumatic events in their lives unless they have to. Most will seek help reluctantly and only when the symptoms of experiencing trauma begin to affect their lives in highly detrimental ways. Typically, people arrive in therapy after having reached the point of desperation, a feeling of nowhere else to turn, and of needing to gain control of their symptoms or salvage aspects of their lives that have become unbearable. They rarely come in eagerly looking forward to talking about the aspects of their lives that are the most troubling even though it can be a relief to do so.

If what drives people into therapy is highly traumatic, it is not always in their best interest to tell the story of the trauma and bring the frightening memories back to the surface. This is a controversial area, as some forms of trauma treatment, such as exposure therapy, involve asking clients to repeatedly tell the story of their trauma until they are desensitized to it. For some, exposure is effective, and for others it is re-traumatizing. For the latter, working through trauma via their dreams takes them a step away from the actual event allowing them to metabolize the painful memories from a safer distance. Symbolic methods of trauma work such as eye movement desensitization and reprocessing (EMDR), art therapy and dreamwork allow those who suffer from the effects of trauma to work from a safer distance through elements of their story that may be forgotten, repressed, stored implicitly because they occurred at a very young age, or were/are too painful to visit in their explicit form.

There are likely many other good reasons to use dreams in the therapy process but overall, the consistent message is that dreams are important to pay attention to because they indicate what really matters to our clients. Dreams are honest and direct us to the heart of matters, so can make the process of therapy richer, deeper and more efficient. For me, dreams have brought the most helpful realizations and catalysts for change in and out of therapy. I have paid attention to them all my life and feel richly rewarded for doing so. And despite my near-death experience, I still like diving into deep waters, both literally and metaphorically.

References

Barrett, D. (2001). *The committee of sleep: How artists, scientists and athletes use their dreams for creative problem solving – and how you can too.* New York, NY: Crown Books/Random House.

Davis, J. L. Byrd, P., Rhudy, J. L., & Wright, D. (2007). Characteristics of chronic nightmares in a trauma-exposed treatment-seeking sample. *Dreaming*, 17(4), 187–198.

Ecker, B. & Hulley, L. (1996). *Depth-oriented brief therapy.* San Francisco, CA: Jossey-Bass Publishers.

Edwards, C., Malinowski, J., McGhee, S., Bennett, P., Ruby, R., & Blagrove, M. (2015). Comparing personal insight gains due to consideration of a recent dream and consideration of a recent event using the Ullman and Schredl dream group methods. *Frontiers in Psychology*, 6, 831.

Ellis, L. A. (2013). Experiential focusing-oriented dream work as a doorway to deeper congruence. *Person-Centered and Experiential Psychotherapies Journal*, 12(3), 274–287.

Ellis, L. A. (2016). Qualitative changes in recurrent PTSD nightmares after focusing-oriented dreamwork. *Dreaming*, 26(3), 185–201.

Eudell-Simmons, E. M. & Hilsenroth, M. J. (2005). A review of empirical research supporting four conceptual uses of dreams in psychotherapy. *Clinical Psychology and Psychotherapy*, 12(4), 255–269.

Freud, S. (1900/2010). *The Interpretation of Dreams.* New York, NY: Basic Books.

Goelitz, A. (2007). Exploring dream work at the end of life. *Dreaming*, 17(3), 159–171. doi: 10.1037/1053-0797.17.3.159.

Hartmann, E. (2001). *Dreams and nightmares: The origin and meaning of dreams.* Cambridge, MA: Perseus Publishing.

Hill, C. E. & Goates, M. K. (2004). Research on the Hill cognitive-experiential dream model. In Hill, C. E. (Ed.), *Dream Work in Psychotherapy: Facilitating Exploration, Insight and Action* (pp. 245–248). Washington, DC: American Psychological Association.

Hill, C. E. & Knox, S. (2010). The use of dreams in modern psychotherapy. In A. Clow & P. Macnamara (Eds.). *International Review of Neurobiology*, 92, Dreams and dreaming (pp. 291–317). Waltham, MA: Academic Press.

Krakow, B., Hollifield, M., Schrader, R., Koss, M., Tandberg, D., Lauriello, J., McBride, L. (2000). A controlled study of imagery rehearsal for chronic nightmares in sexual assault survivors with PTSD: a preliminary report. *Journal of Traumatic Stress*, 13(4), 589–609.

Krakow, B., Hollifield, M., Johnston, L., Koss, M., Schrader, R., Warner, T. D. ... (2001). Imagery rehearsal therapy for chronic nightmares in sexual assault survivors with post-traumatic stress disorder: a randomized controlled trial. *JAMA*, 286(5), 537–545.

Kramer, M. (1991). The nightmare: A failure in dream function. *Dreaming*, 1(4), 277–285.

Leonard, L., & Dawson, D. (2018). The marginalisation of dreams in clinical psychological practice. *Sleep Medicine Reviews*, 42.

Pesant, N. & Zadra, A. (2004). Working with dreams in therapy: What do we know and what should we do? *Clinical Psychology Review*, 24, 489–512.

Sacks, O. (1996). Neurological dreams. In D. Barrett, (Ed.). *Trauma and dreams*, pp. 212–216. Cambridge, MA: Harvard University Press.

Spangler, P. T., & Hill, C. E. (2015). The Hill Cognitive-Experiential Model: an integrative approach to working with dreams. In M. Kramer and M. Glucksman, Eds., *Dream research: Contributions to clinical practice*. New York: Routledge.

Spoormaker, V. I. & van den Bout, J. (2006). Lucid dreaming treatment for nightmares: a pilot study. *Psychotherapy and Pyschosomatics*, 75(6), 389–394.

Taylor, J. (1992). *The wisdom of your dreams: using your dreams to tap into your unconscious and transform your life*. New York, NY: Penguin Group.

Tien, H., Lin, C., & Chen, S. (2006). Dream interpretation sessions for college students in Taiwan: Who benefits and what volunteer clients view as most and least helpful. *Dreaming*, 16(4), 247–257. doi: 10.1037/1053-0797.16.4.246

2 Bringing It Home

Inviting Dreamwork into Your Practice, and Your Life

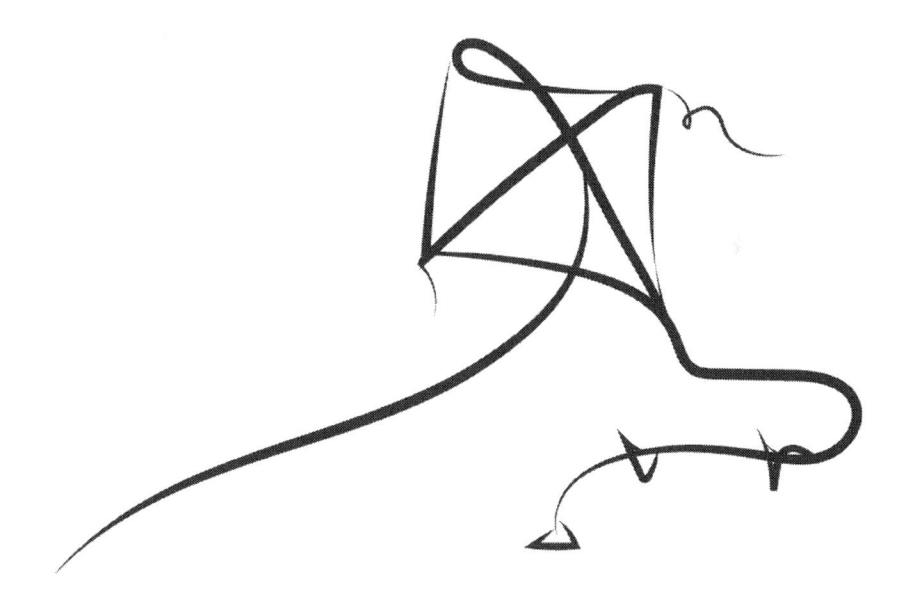

"You know what I mean? Real and unreal, beautiful and strange, like a dream. It got me high as a kite, but it didn't last long enough. It ended too soon and left nothing behind."
That's how it is with dreams," said Priscilla. "They're the perfect crime."

Tom Robbins, *Jitterbug Perfume*

Most often, it is the clients who bring up the topic of dreams in psychotherapy after waking up curious about a particularly strange or moving experience of dreaming. If these initial dreams are welcomed with curiosity and enthusiasm, very likely the client will bring in more dreams. However, in my discussions with therapists about their relationship to dreamwork, I find that many do not feel comfortable working with dreams, and they see this as a missed opportunity. Most view dreams as an opening to explore something with depth and meaning for their clients, but rather than head into unfamiliar terrain, those who feel uncomfortable with dreamwork tend to direct the conversation elsewhere, or refer the dreamwork to another therapist. Neither seems ideal for the client or the therapist. I am hoping, by the end of this book, you will feel more comfortable, maybe even excited, about opening up your practice to include dreamwork.

This chapter will cover the basics of where to begin if you want to support your clients to bring dreams to their sessions. Many of these same techniques can be used to explore your own dreams, a practice that is invaluable for learning the language of dreamwork. In fact, I would suggest that working with your dreams by yourself, or better yet with a group, partner or therapist, is the best way to learn dreamwork and to develop a genuine appreciation for the depth and ingenuity of dreams. What follows is practical information for anyone with an interest in working with their dreams, including how to recall and record them, and something even more basic as a prerequisite to dreaming: getting a good nights' sleep! The current sleep and dream deprivation crisis is explored, along with potential solutions.

Reasons for Therapists to Attend to Our Dreams

There are many good reasons for therapists to engage in their own dreamwork, in addition to working with the dreams of clients. Dreams can be a source of personal growth and insight, a means of self-care, and a source of information about your clients and the therapeutic relationship, pointing to trouble spots you may otherwise miss. Beauchemin (2017) suggests "dreams involving clients can highlight counter-transference issues such as problems in the therapeutic relationship, or vicarious traumatization." I would add that doing your own dreamwork is the best way to develop an appreciation for the dreams themselves and gain a more instinctive feel for how to navigate the dream worlds of your clients. Sometimes your dreams and those of your clients will offer comment on the clinical situation quite directly.

I have had a number of dreams over the years that have referred to my clients. A common theme involves me and the client tending to a baby or a child, which can be seen as a metaphor for our therapy work with early childhood memories, or those child-like aspects we have been attending to in therapy. The dreams involving clients have not always been good news – sometimes there is a sense we are rescuing or comforting these dream children, but sometimes they are in distress, or the form of help we are offering is not working. Dreams have shown me a way forward when the therapy has reached an impasse, or have depicted a source of strength in the client that I did not know was there. While typically I would not share such dreams directly with my client, many of them do prompt me to reassess my work with that person in light of aspects of the dream that seem to asking for a course correction. Similar adjustments might also come from clients' dreams about the therapy. For example, my client had a dream that I was helping them clean up their house. They said I did a pretty superficial job and they were left to do all the hard work. But they also dreamt that I helped light up some dark corners in the house they didn't know were there. The metaphorical message here is pretty clear, and the dream prompted a wonderfully honest conversation about the ways the therapy was and was not working for this client.

Recalling and Recording Dreams

When I mention that I work with and write about dreams, often the first thing people say is, "I don't dream." Or sometimes, more accurately, "I never remember my dreams." Most of us dream what is in essence a feature film worth of dreams every night, but the vast majority of these nocturnal movies are not merely forgotten, but not laid down as accessible memories in the first place. Dreams reside in implicit memory and most of them slip back into this unconscious realm before we have a chance to catch them. But there are some reliable ways to improve your dream recall.

Have you ever noticed that the vast majority of your dreams are not finished? They tend to end right in the middle of something that is striking or scary enough to wake you up. This may be one of the reasons dreams tend to have such a flamboyant way of expressing themselves – it often takes something quite dramatic for a dream to break through to consciousness. And there are some dreams that are so vivid and engaging, we wake up with their images still resonating in our minds and bodies. Still, it takes a deliberate effort to recall even some of the most fascinating dreams. Many dreamers have the experience of a stunning dream that wakes them up. They think, "Wow, this is something I will not forget," only to find that by morning all they remember was the experience of having had a big dream but not the dream itself.

Our most vivid, emotionally toned and complex dreams happen later in the sleep cycle, toward morning. I find that if you are able to wake up naturally and have some time to linger in the dream world before you leap out of bed and start your day, you have a better chance of catching hold of your dream before it slips away. If you lie very still when you first wake up, the dream is more likely to stay with you. And if you rehearse it in your mind a few times and then write it down before you get on with the business of your day, you will find that you have not only captured this dream, but others will come. If you don't have the luxury of extra time in the morning, it can even help to jot down a few key images about a dream because that can jog your memory and bring the entire dream back with it. The sooner you can write the dream out, the more detail you will recall. A little sketch can also be very helpful as dreams are most often visual and convey spatial information. Having a dream journal handy beside the bed is both a way of inviting dreams to come, and a reliable way of capturing them in a timely fashion, as some can slip away quickly.

Generally once a person starts writing their dreams down and paying attention to them, more come. When we pay attention to our dreams, it as if they respond back to us. I have worked with psychotherapy clients' dreams for more than 20 years and found that even those who profess not to dream were able to recall dreams more frequently as we talked about dreams and began working with the dreams they did bring. At first people who don't profess to dream much might capture only a snippet or two and not think much of it. But even little scraps of image can reveal themselves to be significant if they are inquired into with deep curiosity and respect.

When I meet with new clients, one of the things I do that invites dreams is simply to tell them dreamwork is a part of how I like to practice. I ask them to make a point of writing down and bringing any dreams they have, especially those they find striking. When they tell me they never recall dreams, I tell them that because of the conversation we just had, dreams may start coming, and often they do. There is tremendous variability in dream frequency and intensity. Some recall enough dream material in such rich detail, it would take too long and be impractical to write it all down every day. I ask these dreamers to bring the dreams that stand out the most or pique their curiosity. Some people hardly dream at all, and I don't belabor the request for dreams, but take them as they come. And for many, dreams come in phases and appear more frequently during times of transition and intensified emotion. Over time, people's dream lives follow themes. Because of this, it is possible for you and your client to gain a mutual familiarity with their particular dream landscape. This deepens the work and also marks life transitions and internal changes. Significant change in dream life can be seen as an accurate gauge of progress in the course of therapy because dreams come from outside of the client's habitual viewpoint, bringing in missing pieces and correcting some of the distortions we all bring to our subjective experiences.

Working with Dreams, Both in and out of Therapy

Sometimes, the feeling or message a dream brings is abundantly clear. A dream can fill you up with a delicious feeling that you can return to throughout your day. With some of my most troubled clients, I have borne witness to some amazing dreams that featured a character or animal that provided deep comfort or uplifting energy right when they needed it most. Sometimes after a person has died, the deceased person will appear in the dreams of those most deeply missing them, and will offer comfort and reassurance. These are all examples of dreams that require no interpretation, but are meant to be experienced and appreciated. They come as gifts.

Other dreams can be an utter mystery to the dreamer. I can vouch for the fact that having a lot of knowledge about dreams does not help in such cases. I have worked with dreams extensively and still have huge blind spots with respect to my own dreams. I believe we can begin the work of tending to our own dreams by writing them down, considering them, and it can really help illuminate aspects of the dream to draw sketches of them. You can also use the focusing method (Gendlin, 1986) of "bias control," which is explained later in this chapter as a way to avoid the common pitfalls of interpreting a dream based on what we already know and believe. We can get partway down the road with our dreams on our own, but my sense is that most dreams are meant to be shared and explored with others. This interest in the social aspect of dreaming is finding its way into the work of dream scientists, who are beginning to consider social benefits in their theories of the purpose of dreaming. In some cultures, it is the norm to weave dreams into the social fabric of everyday life. I met a Romanian woman recently who said when her mother calls, the first thing she asks about is her dreams, not her waking life. But in modern Western culture, generally dreams are not recalled, told or valued as often as in the past, and sleep itself is being eroded.

The "Silent Epidemic" of Sleep and Dream Deprivation

One of the first and most obvious reasons that, as a culture, we don't dream as well or as often is due to the increasingly poor quantity and quality of our sleep. According to Walker (2018), a full two-thirds of adults in all developed countries do not get a full eight hours of sleep. He lists many adverse health consequences of inadequate sleep: significantly increased risk of cancer, cardiovascular disease, Alzheimer's, depression, anxiety, weight gain and overall, a shortened lifespan. In fact, lack of sleep can literally kill you. Walker cites the existence of a very rare genetic disorder which renders it impossible for the afflicted person to sleep, and after 12 to 18 months, they will die.

There are many reasons for the erosion of our sleep in the developed world. The ideal conditions for a good night's sleep are those that mimic the world before technology. At night it was generally dark, silent and cool. The fading light and dropping temperature signal the body to increase melatonin levels in preparation for sleep. Walker suggests that even the slightest glow from a night light can hamper this process, and screen time right before bed can delay the body's sleep-preparation processes by hours. Taking a pill or having a drink may seem like the answer, but in fact makes matters worse, as both adversely affect the quality of sleep.

Walker said that part of the reason we have devalued sleep is that scientists were, until recently, unable to determine a function for sleep. What has emerged is that there are many functions for sleep and dreaming, and in fact,
"we are now forced to wonder whether there are *any* biological functions that do not benefit by a good night's sleep ... Sleep is the single most effective thing we can do to reset our brain and body health each day."

Due mainly to the availability of artificial light, we sleep an average of four hours less each day than our ancestors did, and most of us also cut off our natural morning sleep with alarm clocks. At times, many of us suffer from those nights when sleep does not come easily, where we toss and turn for hours, unable to shut down our mind. However, the most common form of sleep deprivation is in fact, early waking. The problem with cutting off this tail end of the sleep continuum is that the last two hours of sleep are the concentrated period of REM, which cycles into our sleep patterns in increasing increments, four or five times a night. Waking early cuts off the longest episode of this dream-rich part of our sleep cycle, which is implicated in the regulation of mood and consolidation of memory.

Beyond Sleep Deprivation to REM/Dream Loss

Naiman (2017), who runs the Centre for Integrative Medicine at the University of Arizona, has suggested that there is a silent epidemic not just of sleep deprivation, but of dream deprivation, that is wreaking havoc on our physical and mental health.

> We are at least as dream deprived as we are sleep deprived. Many of the health concerns attributed to sleep loss result from a silent epidemic of REM sleep deprivation. REM/dream loss is an unrecognized public health hazard that silently wreaks havoc with our lives, contributing to illness, depression, and an erosion of consciousness.

In his article, "Dreamless," Naiman lists the many factors that contribute to the loss of dreaming in our culture.

> These include (1) substances, especially alcohol and cannabis; (2) REM-sleep suppressive prescriptions and over-the-counter (OTC) medications; (3) major sleep disorders, including insufficient sleep syndrome; (4) lifestyle factors that interfere with REM/dreaming; and (5) indirectly, a dismissive attitude about the value and meaning of dreams.

Part of the problem is that most of the substances Naiman lists as leading to reduced REM/dreaming are those that people routinely take help them sleep. Alcohol, for example, helps people fall asleep faster, but overall it leads to poorer-quality sleep and disrupted REM. Popular over-the-counter sleep medications may seem to aid in better sleep but in fact, Naiman said they usually alter the architecture of sleep, sacrificing deep sleep for increased light sleep. Antidepressants of all types suppress REM sleep. Although there is some evidence that links excessive REM sleep with depression, Naiman suggests that in fact, this extra dreaming "may well be part of an endogenous healing process to restore previously suppressed REM/dreams." This phenomenon is known as *REM rebound*, which refers to the increase in REM following a period of REM sleep deprivation. The body attempts to catch up on the REM that it missed, which indicates how important REM/dream sleep must be to our health and well-being.

What are the consequences of REM/dream deprivation? One of the consequences Walker (2018) discovered through research is that we see the world as more hostile. When deprived of sleep, study participants

> slipped into a default of fear bias, believing even gentle or somewhat friendly looking faces were menacing. The outside world had become a more threatening and aversive place when the brain lacked REM sleep – untruthfully so. Reality and perceived reality were no longer the same in the 'eyes' of the sleepless brain. By removing REM sleep, we had, quite literally, removed participants' levelheaded ability to read the social world around them.

Naiman extends the benefit of dreaming beyond health and social benefits to include the spiritual realm. He advocates for a change in our biases against the dream world:

> Great philosophers have warned that we routinely mistake the limits of our personal perception for the limits of the universe. Nowhere is this rudimentary error more evident than in our posture toward REM/dreaming. We typically approach and investigate the dream from a biased, wake-centric perspective. Much like the ethnocentrism of early anthropologists, we presume that waking consciousness is the norm and view dreaming as a secondary, subservient state of consciousness. Wake centrism casts our dream experiences as weird and meaningless and discourages us from getting near, let alone going through, the looking glass.

Naiman is not alone in advocating for increased valuing of dreams for their own sake and on their own terms. I have noticed that people who routinely spend time with their dreams tend to shift toward this more expansive and spiritual direction, as though the dreams themselves bring about this change. Although most scientific inquiry into our relationship with dreams focuses on their impact on waking life experience, Naiman said his clinical work has led him to consider dreaming from more of a transpersonal perspective:

> REM/dream loss might erode the breadth of our consciousness, potentially dampening creativity, impairing social connection, and compromising our spirituality. Four decades of clinical dream work has taught me that REM/dreaming is essentially another way of seeing – a kind of transpersonal dream eyesight. By providing us with a novel, wide-angled view of ourselves and the world, dream eyes restore our peripheral vision.

Naiman offers some basic practices to enhance REM/dreaming: manage substance and medication use, optimize sleep using good sleep hygiene practices, properly use dream-enhancing substances like melatonin, share and talk about dreams, even (especially) the bad ones, and generally spend time with your dreams. He also suggests a new diagnostic category for REM/dream loss that could lead to an increase in meaningful research in this area, and supporting broader public education about the health and societal benefits of dreaming.

To sum up, our dream lives are shrinking because we don't attend to and value our dreams enough. Naiman believes that to change this, we need to more deeply consider our dreams from their own perspective. This echoes Hillman (1979), who suggests we do violence to the dream when we try to take it out of its natural "underworld" realm and translate it into a day-world perspective. In my practice, I have shifted toward this transpersonal direction, but also can still see the value in considering the dream, at least in part, in relationship to waking life.

It may be that many levels operating are at once within the dream, as Jung originally suggested – a progression from personal to collective or archetypal. In learning to embrace dreams, especially for those who are skeptical, it may be a case of taking small steps. The first is to recognize, at the very least, that dreams and REM sleep are critical to our mental health. Taking it a step further, they can become a helpful guide in personal life situations. And yet further, they can foster and mediate our relationship with the divine.

One Way to Work with Your Own Dreams: Bias Control

It is difficult to work with your own dreams, and in any case, it serves a social purpose to tell your dreams to others, increasing intimacy and empathy on the part of both the dreamer and the listener. However, there is a method that was devised specifically for personal dreamwork by Gendlin (1986) called *bias control*. As the name indicates, the method is designed to account for the bias we bring to our own dreams, and to life in general: the tendency to see things the way we believe them to be. When we interpret our own dreams this way, we are making meaning that reinforces what we already know, or we are simply mystified by our dream. Bias control is similar to Jung's notion of dreams as compensatory. It simply asks the dreamer to attend to the place(s) in the dream that they dislike, disagree with or are even repelled by, and to consider how such aspects might live inside themselves.

There is a similar step that can be made in waking life to help unearth unconscious projections. When we, or our clients, are repelled by a character trait or action and the emotional response is far out of proportion to the event, it is an invitation for self-reflection. This aversion, whether in dream elements or in life, is an indication (to use another term from Jung, 1969) that a *complex* is being touched upon. A complex is a feeling-toned constellation of experience in a particularly sensitive area of our lives. It tends to crop up because it has not been fully processed or brought into conscious awareness. Often the reason for such a big reaction is that the offending dream element has touched a tender spot inside that we tend to avoid. Rather than sitting with the uncomfortable truth that this anger, greed, vanity or whatever the dream is presenting that we abhor actually lives inside of us, we project it onto others and/or the characters in our dreams. Turning toward what seems aversive in our own dreams can bring discomfort and ultimately, self-knowledge, humility and growth. This is also an effective technique that can be tactfully used for working clinically with client dreams. In fact, as you will see in the final chapter, being contrarian in doing dreamwork and juxtaposing contradictory elements has the strongest potential to be transformational.

References

Beauchemin, K. (2017). Through the looking glass: Reflecting on counsellor dreams for enhanced self-care and effective practice. *International Journal for the Advancement of Counselling*, Sept. 2017. Springer.

Gendlin. E. T. (1986). *Let your body interpret your dreams*. Willmette, OR: Chiron Publications.

Hillman, J. (1979). *The dream and the underworld*. New York, NY: HarperPerennial.

Jung, C.G. (1969). *The structure and dynamics of the psyche*. Collected Works, 8. Princeton, NJ: Princeton University Press.

Naiman, R. (2017). Dreamless: The silent epidemic of REM sleep loss. *Annals of the New York Academy of Sciences*.

Walker, M. (2018). *Why we sleep: Unlocking the power of sleep and dreams*. New York: Scribner.

3 Common Factors
Toward a Universal Approach to Working with Dreams

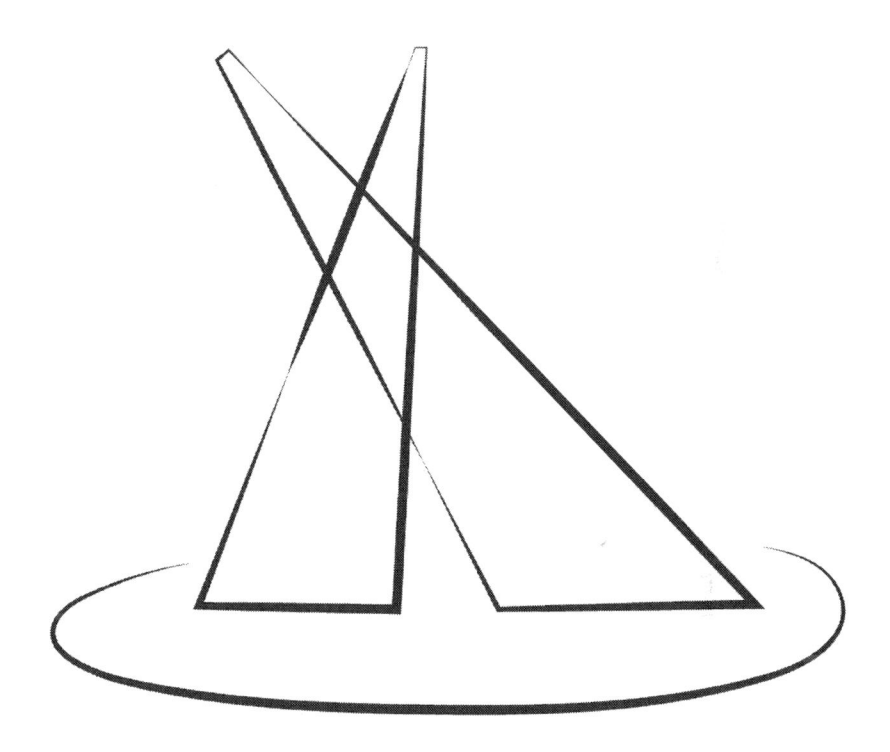

I suppose it is submerged realities that give to dreams their curious air of hyper-reality. But perhaps there is something else as well, something nebulous, gauze-like, through which everything one sees in a dream seems, paradoxically, much clearer. A pond becomes a lake, a breeze becomes a storm, a handful of dust is a desert, a grain of sulphur in the blood is a volcanic inferno. What manner of theater is it, in which we are at once playwright, actor, stage manager, scene painter and audience?

W.G. Sebald, *The Rings of Saturn*

28 *Common Factors*

Is there a simple and universal way to work with dreams? This was one of the guiding questions in the writing of this book. In spite of their multi-faceted complexity, to which Sebald (1998) so eloquently refers, all dreams can be approachable with an attitude of respect, curiosity and a willingness to learn. Like many therapists who have worked with dreams in clinical practice for a very long time (in my case, more than 20 years), I have developed a personal approach that has its foundation in the formal training I received, but which has been augmented over the years by additional training and further shaped by interaction with clients. My initial dreamwork training is Jungian, from the school of archetypal psychology, which is more embodied and experiential than some of the more intellectual branches of Jungian analysis. Over the years, I have added to and subtracted from this theoretical base, as many therapists do; we are lifelong learners because our profession demands this.

Very early in my career as a therapist, I added a focusing approach which deepened the embodied aspects of my dreamwork practice, and moved it away from some of the traditional theoretical constructs that presume certain things about a dream before truly inquiring into it. For example, I now no longer assume, as a typical Jungian might, that every major opposite-sex figure in a dream represents the anima/animus archetypes so central to Jungian dream theory. Over time, we therapists become more eclectic, picking up what serves us and dropping those aspects of our training that become replaced by newer ideas or no longer represent what we believe is helpful or relevant to our clients. Jung himself alluded to this and suggested we need a to develop a new therapy practice for each and every client that comes through our office door.

Mapping Common Pathways of Dreamwork

Scattered throughout this book are many clinical examples from my practice and from others', and I have also included examples of my personal sampling of various dreamwork practices. The examples from my clinical practice show how my method has evolved to become mainly Jungian/focusing-oriented, with a heavy sprinkling of Gestalt practices. Underlying this, and all clinical dreamwork, are some of Freud's enduring ideas about the unconscious and the value of inquiring into dreams. What I propose to readers is not to adopt my way, but to use this book as a guide to find your own way to work with dreams, picking up what makes sense to you from your own theoretical perspective, and setting aside anything that does not feel like a natural or effective way for you to work with your clients' dreams. In service to this idea, I spent about six months doing research to determine the common factors in modern dreamwork. My guiding question was simply: what are the specific practices common to the dreamwork methods most in use today? In this chapter, I will tell you exactly what I did in my attempt to answer this question, and provide the results. In this book, I will give you a practical sense of how to use each of these methods – which I am presuming are popular across theories and modalities because so many therapists have found them to be effective. It's a bit like getting the greatest hits of modern Western dreamwork practices.

I will cut to the punch line and not leave you in suspense. After a detailed qualitative analysis of two current texts that cover the basics of most major approaches to dreams, I found almost unanimous support for experiential approaches to dreamwork, and a very distinct move away from all forms of interpretation by the dreamworker. This came as a surprise to me, albeit a pleasant one because it happens to align with my own way of working with dreams. But I had truly expected more of a balance between those who would offer dream interpretations, and those who would leave this up to the dreamer. After all, interpretation by the therapist is the way clinical dreamwork began, in particular with Freud, who felt confident one could interpret a dream text without any input from the dreamer. Times have definitely changed.

Common Factors in Context

Before I get to the specific outcome of my research, I will provide a bit of background about the idea of common factors research. In the field of psychotherapy, 30 years and 60,000 studies later, it has been determined that all "bona fide, theory-driven" approaches (Lambert, 2013) have been shown to work equally well. Or to quote the dodo bird in *Alice in Wonderland*, "Everyone has won and all must have prizes!" So rather than investing a lot more time and research effort pitting one modality against another, there is a progressive movement toward identifying common factors – specific practices such as attending to the quality of the therapeutic alliance – that can be shown to improve clinical outcomes regardless of the modality used. The study I conducted identifies such common factors in clinical work with dreams (Ellis, 2019).

The main text I used for the qualitative research project was *Working with Dreams and PTSD Nightmares: 14 Approaches for Psychotherapists and Counselors* (Lewis & Krippner, Eds., 2016). This was chosen because it is the most current and complete survey of Western dreamwork methods. It's mission is to provide therapists with a practical sense of how to use each given method, so it features detailed methodological descriptions and clinical examples well-suited to my analysis. I also added Bulkeley's (1997/2017) *An Introduction to the Psychology of Dreaming* to my analysis because it provides a clear, concise survey of all of the traditional dreamwork methods, offers additional perspective and adds detail I felt was missing from some of the methodological descriptions in the Lewis and Krippner book.

Qualitative research involves the laborious process of going over the text under review line by line and "coding" the material based on themes that you either predetermine or add to a list as they arise when you progress through the text. My mission was to highlight and categorize every single instance where a specific dreamwork method was explained or used in an example, and thus to identify all the specific dreamwork practices used in all the methods surveyed. I used the software NVivo, which automates the process of counting all the references, and once I had combed through the texts a couple of times, I also used the software to sort all the methods into logical overarching categories. If you have done any qualitative research, you can appreciate what a time-consuming and immersive process this is. At the end of it all I was rewarded with a pleasant surprise: results that showed a dramatic change in the way dreamwork is now practiced, a clear trend toward experiential approaches to the dream.

The following are the conclusions I arrived at on the basis of my research so far, although I can see there is a lot more that could be done to add detail to the dreamwork practices and ensure the mix of modalities examined is truly representational. My sense is that the main common factors will not alter much as more data is gathered, but that further research could help to flesh out, order, refine and accurately proportion the rich mix of dreamwork methods represented here.

A Clear Trend toward Experiential Methods

What I concluded at the end of my study is that there is a distinct trend toward experiential methods as the main way of working with dreams. The most popular experiential techniques include telling the dream as if it is happening in the present, dreaming the dream onward, and inviting the dreamer to enter into the subjective experience of a dream character or element. The surprising part was there was almost total consensus that the dreamworker refrain from interpretation of the dream. Instead there was an emphasis on collaborative exploration with the dreamer, and a focus on exploring the emotional landscape of the dream. Most of the dreamwork modalities reviewed also suggest the dreamworker adopt an attitude of not-knowing, setting aside or bracketing out preconceptions based on theoretical orientation. The dreamer is viewed as the expert of their dream.

The following is part of the conclusion of my common factors research article regarding the end goals of dreamwork:

> In terms of outcomes of dreamwork, making waking-life connections, understanding the metaphors in the dream and engendering insight or new growth were seen as the most important results of the process. Solving problems or taking action as a result of the dreamwork were considered important in some methods as well.
>
> (Ellis, 2019)

From the common factors research, I gleaned most of the topics that form the content of this book; the list includes all of the specific dreamwork methods that have been adopted by the majority of modern dreamwork protocols. I have woven the techniques into a structure that is intended to feel like a journey, and to mimic the way one might meander through a dream, following one's curiosity and braving the unknown. I will describe, with examples, all of the common factors, and sketch out a map for you to follow as a dreamworker. The main highway will include the practices that are the most common factors, the obvious first step being the simple telling of the dream, which of course is used in all methods.

Where the path diverges, which method you choose in your dream exploration with clients will depend on your own philosophy of dreamwork, which this book will help you arrive at or clarify if you haven't done so already. For example, one of the main philosophical divides concerns the use of projections onto the dream by someone other than the dreamer, which is central to the major group dreamwork methods and yet is a technique to be avoided at all costs in other approaches. A major practical divide can be found between those who would explore the dream on its own terms, and those who would focus on making connections between the dream and waking life with the goal of gaining personal insight and direction. And for some, such approaches are not mutually exclusive, but instead the former leads to the latter.

The following is the list of steps I have proposed for a generic dreamwork approach that includes the specific methods favored by the broadest array of approaches from among the ones studied. It is not intended to be definitive, but rather a genuine attempt to update and simplify dreamwork by condensing it down to the essential steps currently in wide practice. I acknowledge that some of the dreamwork methods surveyed in my qualitative analysis are themselves already a collection of best practices (i.e. Hill Method, Focusing, and Integral). This proposed generic method is meant to be as inclusive as possible and transparent about the theory underlying the specific techniques included to allow for choice points depending on therapist orientation and the clinical situation, which may differ even within one person's practice. For example, I do ask for group members' projections when I'm teaching dreamwork in a group and want to demonstrate how much depth and richness can come from what may appear at first to be a small, rather insignificant dream. But I very rarely offer my projections in a one-on-one dreamwork session because for me it makes sense to help the dreamer stay as close as possible to the dream itself and their own responses to it.

Dreamwork strikes me as a dance that blends leading and following – and in a typical clinical dyad, I see myself as the one who knows the basic steps, but I see the dreamer and their dream as the ones directing the dance. When in doubt, I try to ask myself what feels most true to the dream itself as evidenced by the reactions of the dreamer. And because my main orientation is focusing, I always gauge this reaction by the way the dreamwork affects their bodily felt sense. The main priority in other methods may be translating the inspiration from the dream into a concrete change or action in life, facilitating the dawning of insight into a difficult aspect of emotional life, a working out of developmental issues, or a spiritual preparation for death. The method of dreamwork used may depend at least as much on what the dreamer is seeking and the kinds of dreams they bring to therapy as it does on the dreamworker's theoretical orientation. So feel free to take the following menu of methods as a starting point to add to or subtract from as suits your dreamwork practice. You may find that your preferred ways of working change as your depth of knowledge and experience increases.

A Proposed Generic Dreamwork Method Based on Common Factors

> Tell the dream
> Explore the setting, including the emotional landscape
> Ask into associations

Experiential exploration of dream elements
Explore metaphorical and other connections to waking life
Name and explore new insights and growth steps

Optional Avenues

Amplification using symbol or myth
Art or creative expression
Reformulation to generic terms
Compensation
Story or plot structure
Finding help in the dream
Pursuing/exploring lucidity
Group projections onto the dream
Action step, life change, new creation or direction

These steps can be used in any order, other than the first one or two. Telling the dream will always be the first step, and exploring the setting is often a good place to begin exploring the dream because it is an easy way to begin and can provide a sense of the dream's context. The above steps also include the addition of one specific suggestion that did not come from the common factors research, that of working with the dreamer to locate and embody the life force or "help" in the dream, a step from focusing dreamwork. I am hoping the overall method feels flexible and open-ended enough for all those interested in working with dreams to try on, adapt, make your own and reject specific aspects as you see fit.

Defining the Steps

The following is a brief definition and explanation of the basic steps outlined above. Throughout this book, the most prevalent methods introduced here will be fleshed out in more detail and supported by clinical examples. My intent is to give enough practical information to provide a clear sense of some of the ways these methods can be incorporated into practice. Or where that isn't possible because the technique represents an entire philosophy and set of steps that are unique to the method, such as lucid dreaming, I will introduce the method briefly.

Tell the Dream

In the common factors research, the striking thing about this category was that all of those who specifically mentioned a method for obtaining the dream report suggested asking the dreamer to reexperience the dream as they were telling it. One way to do this is to ask the dreamer to speak in first person and present tense. Another way is to ask the dreamer to bring their attention back into the atmosphere of the dream, and try to re-enter the dream scene using as many senses as possible. It will be clear that the dream re-entry is successful when the dreamer can look around and see details that were previously not available to their memory. If the dreamer has the dream written down, I ask them to read the text as written to jog their memory and ensure otherwise-forgotten details are included. But then I usually ask them to re-tell it experientially, walking through the dream again and describing the experience as fully as possible from memory.

Explore the Setting, including the Emotional Landscape

This process will be easier if the dreamer has been telling the dream from inside it. The landscape will then feel very present and alive, and they will be able to describe it in detail – provided the original dream setting was rich in detail, though not all of them are. The feeling in the dream is also part of the setting. Often the mood in the dream carries important information that gets lost unless it is inquired about directly.

Ask for Associations to the Dream

This method, which originated with Freud's method of free association, is used in all but one dreamwork modality, although to considerably varying degrees. Most dreamworkers ask for associations to various dream elements early on in the process – sometimes to map out the memory sources of the dream, and sometimes as a way to link the dream scenario to waking life concerns. Some methods, such as Gestalt, suggest keeping association to a minimum in favor of staying close to the dream images themselves.

Experiential Exploration of Dream Elements

There are many possible ways to experientially explore a dream. The most popular way is to invite the dreamer to be a dream character or element, to revisit the dream from the perspective of the most interesting, or perplexing character or element in the dream. You can use any dream element for this purpose, not just people in the dream but also animals or inanimate objects. Some methods also suggest engaging in a dialogue or interaction with a dream character. The other popular experiential method is to enter the dream at the end, or at any point that feels unresolved, and allow the dream to continue on from there.

Explore Metaphorical and Other Connections to Waking Life

Many dreamworkers understand dreams as speaking the language of picture-metaphor that depicts an emotional situation in the dreamer's life. When this is the case, the dream is not taken at literal face value but seen as an apt representation in terms that may make sense only to the dreamer. This makes the dreamwork a bit like detective work as the process of discovery uncovers the dream's message. In this type of approach, the dreamer's bloody murder of the policeman, for example, may speak to the end of the dreamer being dominated by authority figures or might suggest they need to kill off the part of themselves that always needs to follow the rules. The former example assumes the dream might be a metaphor for aspects of the dreamer's life, while the latter views the dream elements as personal aspects of the dreamer. Both are popular and valid ways of working. Only the dreamer can say for sure, but this search for the meaning behind the dream metaphors can be one of the most rewarding and fun aspects of dreamwork.

Consider What New Insights or Personal Growth Steps Come from the Dream

Once the connections have been made between the dream elements and their memory sources or metaphorical representation of a life situation, personal insight often dawns on the dreamer without any further prompting. Such a process often leads to change, and sometimes to a sense of what concrete new actions might be taken as a result of the dream. The Hill method, for example, includes a specific step for discussing what the dreamer might actually do differently in response to the dream.

Optional Avenues

In this part of the dreamwork process, we arrive at many more choice points. My general practice is to inquire into the dream elements in roughly chronological order on the first pass through the dream so as not to miss anything. As you will see in some of the examples in this book, sometimes the small, seemingly-insignificant details can turn out to be important keys to the dream's meaning. After I have walked through the dream once with the dreamer, I will then look for the helpful places in the dream, followed by an exploration of those elements the dreamer is most curious about, and then ask the dreamer to consider places in the dream that I think might be important but that seem to have been missed. It is quite common for the dreamer to miss important elements in their own reading of the dream because dreams are often about our blind spots or about things we repress, and this same repression or bias continues when we work with our own dream material. It's one reason why it so helpful to have a therapist, partner or group to do dreamwork with.

Amplification Using Symbol or Myth

This method is from Jung and his theory that dreams have their source not only in our personal experience, but also the collective experience of being human. He called the enduring patterns of human experience archetypes, and found that these universal elements often show up not only in our most important dreams, but also in myths and legends recorded throughout human history. Many Jungians make it a practice to look for material in the dream that may relate to enduring myths, particularly when the dream does not seem to make sense from a purely personal perspective. Some cultures believe that all dreams are collective and meant to be shared with the larger community; the idea that they are purely personal is a more recent one most prevalent in Western culture.

Art or Creative Expression

Creatively depicting or enacting one's dream through art or other forms of expression is also an idea made popular by Jung, and it has been widely adopted. One reason for this is that dreams tend to be visual and spatial, so creating an image of the dream can be a more direct and accurate depiction of its contents. There is also more room for the unconscious to continue to express itself through art, and a way that artistic expression can be used to honor or respond to the dream. (See Chapter 9 for examples.)

Reformulation to Generic Terms

This method refers to a specific way of decoding the dream to flesh out the metaphors inherent in many dreams. Some methods, such as the Dream Interview method, rely heavily on this technique, which operates on the assumption that dream material is made up of personal metaphors for our life situation and that decoding these will give us the key to our dream's meaning. For example, following the Dream Interview technique, if someone dreamt about driving an old sports car with their spouse, the first question might be: "I'm from outer space. What is a sports car?" For one person, it might be a coveted luxury item, for another, an unreliable or impractical way of getting where you're going. Let's say it's the latter, and that the dreamer is a woman whose husband is driving the car recklessly. Such a dream could be a metaphor for the way the dreamer experiences their partner in relationship – it might be saying that they feel their partner is unreliable, and is thus being reckless with the marriage. You can see that the dreamer's own personal association is critical here, and also how this way of exploring dream images can open up the exploration into areas of relevance that at first may not have been apparent.

Compensation

This is another idea from Jung, who viewed dreaming as compensatory. In his autobiography, *Memories, Dreams, Reflections,* Jung (1965) shared a personal experience of a dream he understood as compensating for his incorrect conscious attitude. He dreamt that his female client was in a tower looking down on him from a great height. It made him realize he had been looking down on her in their analytic interactions, and when he shared the dream with her, the process, which had stalled, moved forward again. In focusing, there is a technique Gendlin (1986) called *bias control* that is designed to help the dreamer experience the compensating elements in the dream, by simply imagining what it would be like to be the dream character that feels so foreign or aversive. For example, the self-effacing woman dreams of a stuck-up princess; imagining herself as the princess she vehemently disliked bolstered her sense of herself as deserving and assertive.

Story or Plot Structure

This technique suggests looking at the overall movement of the dream as a story as it relates to the dreamer's life. To do this, simply strip the dream report down to the bare bones of the narrative and ask the dreamer if anything in their life reminds them of that. For example, I had a dream the other night in which I was a passenger in a vehicle that was barreling down a mountain road way too fast, and I could steer it but not slow it down. Since this is my dream, I can simply ask myself, is there anything in my life with a basic story like that, something I can steer but not slow down? It makes me laugh because my whole life feels like that runaway vehicle sometimes, and so many people I talk to can relate to this feeling. (More on this dream later.)

Finding Help in the Dream

This is a step I am including from focusing dreamwork, even though it did not emerge as a common factor in the study. I am adding it as a step here because it has proven so helpful in my dreamwork practice. I consider finding help similar to resourcing a client prior to trauma work – when a client is invited to find a sense of strength and calm before working with difficult places, more opens up than was otherwise possible. Finding help is the practice of seeking and embodying the places in the dream that feel alive and positive, such as animals, children, plants or anything beautiful and/or uplifting. (For more on finding help, see Chapter 8.)

Pursuing/Exploring Lucidity

In the text surveyed for common factors, there were two kinds of lucidity mentioned by the authors. The most commonly understood form of lucidity is the awareness that you are dreaming while you are still dreaming. This can happen spontaneously or be cultivated as a skill that can deepen over time. Lucidity can take many forms. Degrees of lucidity run along a continuum from simple awareness that yes, this is a dream at one end of the spectrum, to the dreamer having a high degree of control over the dream and their actions within it at the other. Lucidity can also be taught, and reliably induced in a laboratory setting, and there is currently an enormous surge of interest in lucid dreaming in all its forms. The other form of lucidity that arose is more like the experiential step of dream reentry, where the dreamer enters the dream landscape while awake and interacts with their dream further.

Group Projections onto the Dream

Offering projections, one's own associations, thoughts and feelings about another person's dream, is a technique most often used in group dreamwork. This practice was made popular in the Ullman (2006) method of group dreamwork where a central part of the process, once the dream has been recited and clarified, is to open the floor to the participants to share their own responses to the dream.

In this method, the participants are asked to preface their comments with, "If this were my dream …" and are not to look at the dreamer as they speak. That way, the dreamer is more apt to feel free to accept or reject these projections as they see fit. Taylor's (2001) projective dreamwork group process also makes extensive use of projection. To give an example of projection, and its potential drawbacks: *a friend dreams he is high in the mountains on a frozen lake*. I might assume the dream represents solitude, loneliness, and an inhospitable environment. In fact, my friend is an avid back-country skier who considers such a place to be like heaven on earth.

Action Step, Life Change, New Creation or Direction

This step invites the dreamer to consider whether there is an action step, life change or new creation one might make as a result of the dreamwork. This is an integral part of the Hill cognitive-experiential method (1996), and an optional part of many other ways of working. All dreamworkers I surveyed, including Hill herself, suggested caution with this step and warned against dreamers rushing to take action as a result of a dream. Some dreams can evolve over time, and some present contrary points of view, so making decisions based on a single dream may not be advisable.

These brief descriptions of the most popular dreamwork methods and techniques will be woven into a suggested generic method for working with dreams, and will also be presented more thoroughly and with clinical examples throughout the rest of this book.

References

Bulkeley, K. (1997/2017). *An Introduction to the Psychology of Dreaming*. Westport, CT: Praeger.
Ellis, L. A. (2019). Common factors leading to a universal approach to dreamwork: A qualitative analysis. *Dreaming* 29(1), 22–39.
Gendlin, E. T. (1986). *Let your body interpret your dreams*. Wilmette, IL: Chiron Publications.
Hill, C. E. (1996). *Working with dreams in psychotherapy*. New York: Guilford Press.
Jung, C. G.; Aniela Jaffé (1965). *Memories, Dreams, Reflections*. New York: Random House.
Lambert, M. (2013). *Outcome in psychotherapy: The past and important advances. Psychotherapy*, 50(1), 42–51.
Lewis, J. E., & Krippner, S., Eds., (2016). *Working with dreams and PTSD nightmares: 14 approaches for psychotherapists and counsellors*. Santa Barbara, CA: Praeger.
Sebald, W. G. (1998). *The rings of Saturn*. New York: New Directions Books.
Taylor, J. (2001). Group work with dreams: The "Royal Road" to meaning. In K. Bulkeley, (Ed.). *Dreams: A reader on religious, cultural and psychological dimensions of dreaming*. New York, NY: Palgrave, pp. 195–208.
Ullman, M. (2006). *Appreciating dreams: A group approach*. New York, NY: Cosimo-on-Demand.

4 Mapping the Route
The Science of Dreaming

> *Why is it that when you awake to the world of realities you nearly always feel, sometimes very vividly, that the vanished dream has carried with it some enigma which you have failed to solve?*
> Fyodor Dostoyevsky, *The Idiot*

Academic dream research is a world apart from the type of inquiry into dreams that takes place in a therapist's office. While the theories about what dreams are and what purpose they serve have advanced considerably since the days of Freud, there is still lively debate and enduring mystery around the nature of dreams. Researchers apply much more exacting standards of proof to their work than clinicians; such is the nature of academic inquiry. Therapists, on the other hand, entertain only one essential question about their chosen method: does it serve my client? Despite this, I would argue that it is useful to have some knowledge of the assumptions we are making when we work with our clients' dreams, and also to know something about the field of dream research because this body of work can shape, guide and update our interventions. The relatively new field of interpersonal neurobiology has transformed the practice of psychotherapy in the past decade, altering how we understand the causes of psychopathology, the far-reaching effects of trauma, and the nature of the unconscious. Therefore, it stands to reason that the increased understanding we now have of the mind/brain/body would affect how we work with dreams in clinical practice as well.

The first assumption most therapists who work with dreams make is that dreams are meaningful and relevant to the lives of their clients. It might come as a surprise to know that researchers continue to spend a great deal of time on the question of whether dreams bear any relationship to waking life. They have amassed considerable support for what they call the *continuity hypothesis* (e.g., Domhoff, 2011a; Schredl, 2015) which proposes simply that there is continuity between dreams and waking life. Most clinicians who work with dreams take continuity for granted and operate on the assumption that *of course* dreams are relevant to our waking lives. For the most part, dream researchers are not concerned with the question of how dreams can help a person heal from past trauma or gain personal insight, but instead tend to explore the more basic questions about the nature and purpose of dreaming itself. They assume nothing, and explore questions such as whether a dream report truly represents the dream, what kinds of topics people typically dream about and how this differs across age and gender, what characterizes different kinds of dreams, and they even ask the question, "Do dreams exist?"

You can rest assured that yes, dreams do exist. According to Milton Kramer (2015), his studies "support the existence of a dream as a valid experience that occurs during sleep and is extended in time." Much of academic dream research explores questions that clinicians do not concern themselves with either at all or only tangentially. Mostly, clinicians want to know how to approach and explore clients' dreams in a way that is helpful and moves the process of therapy forward. Fortunately, there is also a body of research specifically about the effects of clinical dreamwork, though its scope is limited (see Chapter 1). This is a brief and selective tour of what the world of academic dream research has established about the nature and function of dreaming, with a focus on those aspects most relevant to clinicians.

Dreaming as Another Form of Thought

One of the most highly respected lifetime dream researchers, Ernest Hartmann, summarized his life's work and understanding of dreams in his last book, *The Nature and Functions of Dreaming* (2011). Hartmann came to view dreaming as at one end of a continuum, with focused waking thought at the other extreme, and fantasy and daydreaming in the middle. He described dreaming as "simply one form of mental functioning… not an alien intrusion." Hartmann insisted that dreams are not a separate and distinctly different form of mental activity. However, dreams do have specific characteristics that differ from waking thought based on the properties of the mind while asleep, such as difficulty with memory, quantitative tasks and voluntary control (lucid dreams being the exception here). Hartmann found that daydreams, which are closest to the dreaming end of the spectrum, share many features in common with night dreams. His research shows that scripts of daydreams can be indistinguishable from night dreams, and that daydreams, when influenced by emotion, become even more dreamlike.

The main characteristic that distinguishes dreams from other forms of mental activity, according to Hartmann, is not their occasionally-bizarre content, but their ability to make creative new connections guided by the emotions of the dreamer, a quality that dream researchers refer to as hyper-associativity. Hartmann sees the language of dreams as mainly 'picture-metaphors' similar to the forms of waking thought at the daydreaming end of the spectrum, and he views the main function of dreams as one of integrating new experiences into existing memory systems, a benefit we realize whether we work therapeutically with our dreams or not. He stressed that dreaming is not simply reconsolidating existing memory, but is also weaving in of new material, guided by our most salient emotional concerns. In this respect, a dream always brings something new, and is never merely a replay of the past. In a later chapter, we will delve more deeply into the theories supporting the relationship of dreams and memory consolidation and will find that, as with most theories about dreams, there is support but it is not unequivocal.

What Is the Function of a Dream?

Hartmann's theory about the function of dreaming (as weaving new experiences, guided by emotion, into our existing web of memory made of associative links) is far from the only theory about the purpose of dreaming. Dream researchers generally agree that dreams must serve some adaptive purpose or evolution would have phased them out, although see Flanagan (2001) for an alternative view. In fact, all mammals may dream since they experience the rapid-eye movement (REM) sleep most closely associated with dreaming, and humans have about 90 minutes of REM sleep every night. An experiment by Rechstaffen (1989) deprived rats of REM and found they would die, their homeostatic balance thrown off to such a degree that they could no longer regulate their body temperature. Rats totally deprived of sleep would also die, and in about half the time, but the symptom picture, including weight loss despite almost doubling their food intake, was otherwise the same for both groups. The researchers concluded that sleep in general, and REM sleep in particular, is necessary for thermoregulation and survival.

Does it follow that dreaming itself, which is the one of the main activities during REM sleep, is critical to life? It used to be thought that REM and dreaming were the same, but neuroimaging studies have shown this is not the case. While the majority of dreams, and the most vivid and interesting dreams take place during REM, we also dream in non-REM (NREM) and sometimes do not dream in REM. The initial discovery of REM sleep (Aserinsky & Kleitman, 1953) was greeted with such fervor it spurred an avalanche of research into what scientists then thought would uncover the secrets of sleep and dreaming. The search continues, however. More recently it is being aided by the advances in neuroscience, which have enhanced our understanding of the neural correlates of sleep and dreaming and provided strong clues about what the function(s) of dreams might be.

Theories of Dream Function: Competing or Complementary?

There are three major ideas that have been studied extensively in the search for the purpose of dreaming: dreams as threat simulation, dreams as regulators of emotion, and dreams as consolidating existing and/or new memory. While these theories are often depicted as competitive, it is more probable that dreams serve many functions, and that all of the well-supported theories may be true to some degree. The way we dream may depend on our situation and what is needed at the time.

We will begin with the theories that have suggested dreams serve no adaptive purpose at all. Allan Hobson and Robert McCarley are the infamous Harvard neurophysiologists whose "activation-synthesis theory" (1977) was popularized as the idea that dreams are nothing more than the hallucinations that happen as a result of the brain's random firing due to brain stem activation during sleep. However, McCarley more recently said his theory was not interpreted correctly and has been "a convenient bogeyman" (Oaklander, 2015). McCarley notes that even back when they first developed their theory, they did not suggest dreams are entirely meaningless, but that Freudian ideas about the nature of dreams needed updating in light of their findings. Specifically, they found that the basic physiological processes that generate dreams account for their unusual properties rather than any form of disguise, wish fulfillment or conversion from some unacceptable version of the content that would then need interpreting by a therapist. Dreams are not disguising unacceptable desires, as Freud (1900/2010) suggested, but the result of how during sleep, the brain powers down the executive functioning areas of the prefrontal cortex and increases activation in the lower and mid-brain structures more closely correlated with emotion and imagination.

Domhoff (2011b), who is a proponent of the idea the dreams serve no adaptive purpose, has suggested that the dreaming brain may be a subsystem of the *default mode network* which is what activates (or, more accurately, refrains from de-activating) when we allow our minds to wander and daydream rather than directing our attention to a specific task. Domhoff constructs a convincing case that there is much overlap in the regions of the brain activated during dreaming and in the brain's default mode network. This form of consciousness has several characteristics in common with dreaming – thought processes can be fragmented and unusual, difficult to recall, based on personal concerns, particularly of the immediate past or future, and characterized by vivid simulation, enhanced thought flow and imagery, but reduced cognitive control. Domhoff said that if the neural substrate for dreaming is, as he suggests, a specific subsystem of the default network "the dreams can be seen as a unique and more fully developed form of mind wandering, and therefore as the quintessential cognitive simulation." However, he argues that it does not necessarily follow that dreaming is adaptive in the evolutionary sense. It may be that "the mind dreams simply because it can."

Dream researcher Katja Valli points out that any theory about the purpose of dreaming must make sense in terms of evolution, and the fact that it takes roughly 40,000 years for evolutionary changes in biological function to take place. Therefore, she argues that the purpose of dreaming must be related to biological function of survival or reproduction in a world very different from our own. This is where the *threat simulation theory* (Revonsuo, 2000; Valli, Revonsuo, et al., 2005) might make sense: Valli and Revonsuo argue that threatening scenarios are overrepresented in dreams so that human beings can rehearse threat avoidance, thus increasing chances of survival. While this may be true, when we are presented with a threatening situation in our dreams, more often than not, we don't succeed in evading the threat, so what we are rehearsing is often the ways we fail to escape.

Another well-researched theory of dream function is that dreams regulate our emotions. There are many proponents of this view, beginning with Freud, who suggested dreams dampen emotional charge and are thus "guardians of sleep" (1900/2010). This theory was supported by decade of research by Kramer (1991) who suggested that the 'emotional surge' associated with REM sleep is contained by dreaming, and that nightmares are examples of dreams that fail to do their job because the level of emotion exceeds the dream's capacity for containment.

This notion is both supported and rendered more complex by the work of Cartwright (2010) who conducted extensive research with divorced participants with depression. She found that specific kinds of dreams correlate with recovery. Those who dreamt of their divorce in realistic ways (with negative emotions and set in the past, present and future rather than just in the past) more quickly recovered from the aftermath of divorce than those who didn't dream at all or those whose dreams mostly replayed happier, earlier memories. She also found that depressed dreamers whose pattern of dreaming moved from negative to positive over the course of the night showed improved mood in both the short and long term. These findings were not universal nor truly experimental, and critics of the research suggest the dreams may correlate with, but not create the recovery process (Blagrove, 2011; Malinowski & Horton, 2015).

Cartwright's main conclusion that dreams appear to down-regulate emotion is widely supported. She noted, in particular, that our dreams help us regulate emotions we have repressed or that were intense enough to still be troubling us at the end of the day. Cartwright (2010) wrote:

> This wake-sleep collaboration is how our behavior remains flexible, how we are able to retain new learning and safely negotiate the bumps of unanticipated misfortunes… The bottom line is that without enough dreaming, at the end of the night we are stuck with our unregulated emotional memories.

She stressed that the nocturnal emotion regulation process works well only if we consistently get enough sleep, particularly the REM sleep concentrated at the end of the sleep cycle. If not, we wake up grouchy and sensitive, and over time can develop more serious psychological problems, including anxiety and depression.

Another major theory of dream function is that dreams are implicated in the consolidation of memory. It has been well established that we consolidate memory during sleep, and the case for dreams playing a role in this process has been strengthened over time. The trouble is that historically the fields of sleep and memory research, and the study of dreams did not cross-fertilize. The evidence for dreaming as implicated in memory processes is challenging to obtain because it is so hard to capture actual dreaming in a reliable way. Self-report based on recollections of dreams is several steps away from the actual dream itself; we forget much of what we dream and change it in the telling. But recalled dream reports are all that researchers currently have as a means to determine dream content. Despite this, recent studies have begun to produce a complex picture of how relevant dreaming may be in the formation and evolution of our memories, and how the theories of memory consolidation and emotional regulation might be linked.

Malinowski and Horton (2015) link emotional regulation and memory consolidation. They conducted an extensive review of the mechanisms behind the assimilation of emotions, taking into account the disparate fields of sleep and dream research. What emerged is a complex picture that weaves together much of the current information about emotion, memory and dreaming. The authors propose that out of the myriad events that take place during a typical day, we select information to remember based on its emotional intensity. During sleep, this information is both consolidated into long-term memory and integrated into existing memory, while the emotionality attached to the memory is assimilated and fades over time. It is as if a major purpose of emotion is to tag an event as something important for us to remember, and once this purpose is served, the emotion can attenuate. In dreaming, the elements of memory are separated into fragments and reconstituted in a metaphorical and hyper-associative manner. The effect of this process is that over time, and depending on both life situation and individual temperamental differences, emotions are attenuated during sleep and dreaming, but the associated memories are retained. If the sleep and dreaming processes are working as they should, intense memories lose their emotional charge, but we still retain the information that is most important to us. In their review, Malinowski and Horton stated there was not enough evidence to say the dreaming directly contributes to emotional assimilation because "at this stage we are not able to measure the additional value of dreaming versus not-dreaming to these processes."

Dreams as "Memory Consolidation in Action"

Dreams are elusive to study and evade definitive statements about their nature and function. However, Harvard associate professor of psychiatry Robert Stickgold and his team have amassed a body of evidence implicating dreams in the process of memory consolidation. In his keynote address at the June 2018 meeting of the International Association for the Study of Dreams, Stickgold lamented the lack of crossover between sleep, memory and dream research. He was introduced as the singular person in the world most expert in all three realms. Before I describe the studies that implicate dreams in the process of memory consolidation, I will summarize some of the important ideas Stickgold presented to the various researchers, clinicians and other dream aficionados assembled in Arizona at the dream conference. He begins by simply stating, "Things happen while we sleep. The average person thinks the brain shuts off when you sleep, but the brain is working all night long."

He tells us he is going to talk about sleep and the *evolution* of memory (Stickgold, 2002). This is a deliberate distinction from the *consolidation* of memory, a process discovered more than 100 years ago to show how new, labile memories can be stabilized and laid down in long term memory. However, even consolidated memories continue to evolve and change over our lifetime (unless there is a problem with the process, such as is the case with those whose trauma memories can't be assimilated and remain as clear and detailed as when they were formed, a major symptom of posttraumatic stress disorder).

Stickgold explains dreaming first from a neurophysiological perspective. Our brains are immersed in a different neurochemical bath depending on whether we are awake or asleep, and this neurochemical environment differs across sleep stages. Each stage, from slow-wave to other non-REM to REM sleep, serves a different function. In REM sleep, more acetylcholine is released even than when awake, while serotonin and norepinephrine are completely shut off (which is essentially the opposite of what happens in NREM). "It is the same brain but running a different program." Stickgold noted that the neuromodulator, acetylcholine is critical for new memory formation and that evolution set up REM sleep as the time when hippocampus is primed for new memory encoding. During REM sleep, the dorsolateral prefrontal cortex, which is associated with executive functioning, logical reasoning and impulse control, is dampened down. At the same time all the mid-line limbic structures of the brain, associated with processing emotion, are ramped up. The result, says Stickgold, is a familiar dreamlike experience where you have lots of feeling, but little or no reason or control.

In the research leading up to Stickgold and his colleague Erin Wamsley's landmark discovery, the first relevant question the team asked is whether we replay *episodic* memories in our dreams, those short slices of life experience we recall in detail, including the time, place, activity and the people in it with us. In fact, less than two percent of the dream reports, but possibly none of them, kept all of these elements together. Most dreams retain only one or two essential elements of the current experience, and then weave in other settings, characters or plots to create something entirely new. Stickgold concluded, "It is very rare in dreams that we actually replay our memories. Instead we dream metaphorically, and associatively about what happened, and sometimes very weakly and divergently about what happened."

The next series of experiments involved having participants play the video game Tetris (Stickgold et. al., 2000). The research team found that new learning was incorporated in the dream reports from the first part of the night for the majority of people who were new to that game. Even the five patients who were included in the study who had cognitive disabilities that rendered them unable to retain memory dreamt of Tetris images. This indicated the memory of the experience is in there, just not the ability to recall it, a finding that made the cover of *Science*.

In their series of sleep and memory studies Stickgold's group found that sleep does a lot of valuable and powerful things for memories, stabilizing and enhancing them, as well as enhancing perceptual and motor learning. The studies showed the importance of a full night's sleep, because 80 percent of the benefit is gained if the subjects get both the slow wave sleep characteristic of the first quarter of the night, and the REM sleep most concentrated in the last quarter. Subsequent nights of sleep are too late; you need the sleep the night of the day you learn something new to gain the benefit of sleep-related performance enhancement. To summarize the findings about how important sleep is to memory: Sleep stabilizes simple declarative memories; the experimental group that stayed awake after learning forgets four times more than the sleep group. And sleep does more than stabilize or strengthen memories in a generic way, but can also strengthen a memory based on salience, and it can extract the gist and the general rules of what has been learned so the new learning can be applied in future situations that are relevant.

How is dreaming implicated in these findings? "We have no idea," Stickgold said. "We are split – those working with memory don't also work with dreams. We are either doing a memory study or a dream study and we were afraid to mix them." But this split was joined in the research led by Erin Wamsley (Wamsley & Stickgold 2010, 2011). She and her colleagues developed a maze task where subjects learned to navigate through to find the exit, half of the participants napped and half stayed awake and then they were all tested again. Nappers were about a minute faster on their second attempt to escape the maze, as was expected based on previous studies of a similar design. But Wamsley also collected dream reports, and found that those who slept but did not dream about the maze performed about the same as those that did not sleep at all between tasks. *All* the improvement came from the people who reported dreams related to the maze. The experiment was repeated with subjects sleeping through the night, and the results were similar (Wamsley et. al., 2012).

Those who thought about the maze task and strategized how to tackle it before trying again did not improve, but those who dreamt about it did improve. Interestingly, the dreams were not rehearsals of navigating the maze, but of tangential things like meeting friend in a maze, travelling through bat caves that were maze-like, and hearing the background techno-rap music from the maze test: "Profoundly useless, can we all agree on that?" Stickgold asked.

> Yet these were the subjects that accounted for all the improvement, possibly because as they dream about maze-like things, their whole brain is working on the problem: imagining ways to navigate such problems in the future, searching the past for relevant information… we don't really know.

Nevertheless, these results were ground-breaking. Stickgold said, "We were ecstatic. We were seeing memory consolidation at work."

However, a critical analysis of this study renders the conclusion somewhat less certain (Schoch et. al., 2018). Those who dreamt about the maze test (and there were only four who did) had something else in common besides dramatic improvement – they were also the participants who performed worst on the test initially, so may have been dreaming about it not because they were rehearsing a better performance, but because they were upset at how poorly they did, and their dreams were a result of the emotional response. As well, those who performed worst had nowhere to go but up, while the people who did well had less room for improvement. Schoch and colleagues also noted that the study only addressed NREM sleep and dreams.

In general, the search for an overarching purpose of dreaming has been unsuccessful, but researchers now tend to agree about something much more plausible – that, like sleep, dreaming serves many functions. There is a trend in general in neuroscience to view our brain's design as inherently social, and this view underlies some of the newer ideas about what dreams may be doing. The threat simulation theory has been updated to include social simulation theory (SST), a theory which holds that while dreams remain simulations, they are often rehearsals that help us respond adaptively in a social context (Revonsuo, Tuominen & Valli, 2015). Another recent theory relating to the social purpose of dreams may account for why dreams are so compelling to tell to others. Blagrove and colleagues (2018) suggest that dreams may increase empathy not just in the dreamer, but also in the listener. This is supported by a study that showed dream sharing increases perceived intimacy in couples (Olsen, Schredl & Carlsson, 2013).

One final theory I will mention is that dreams are a form of imaginative play, which may account for both their social and their creative nature. Bulkeley (2004) notes that across species, play revolves around activities important to survival. However, it takes place in an "unreal" space where activities like fighting and defending, conflict resolution, and finding food or mates are not taken quite as seriously. Human beings play more than any other species, and Bulkeley argues that play and dreaming similarly offer an enjoyable, engaging, and sometimes surprising venue to try on different actions and responses. The result is greater adaptive readiness for similar 'real-life' situations.

It appears that the trajectory of dream research and theory is aligning with the paradigm shift in general in psychotherapy that views our human design as relational versus individual. Overall, there is a great deal of research being conducted into the many questions about the nature of dreaming, but similar to the case with the world of sleep and memory research, the clinical research community does not cross-fertilize enough with those who research dreams. It is an area that is ripe for further inquiry.

References

Aserinsky, E., & Kleitman (1953). Regularly occurring periods of eye motility and concurrent phenomena during sleep. *Science*, 118, 273–274.

Blagrove, M. (2011). Distinguishing continuity/discontinuity, function, and insight when investigating dream content. *International Journal of Dream Research*, 4(2), 45–47.

Blagrove, M., Carr, M., Jones, A., & Lockheart, J. (2018). A new theory of dream function: telling dreams enhances empathy for the dreamer. Poster presentation, International Association for the Study of Dreams conference, Scottsdale, AZ.

Bulkeley, K. (2004). Dreaming is play: Revonsuo's threat simulation theory in ludic context. *Sleep and Hypnosis*, 6(3), 119–129.

Cartwright, R. D. (2010). *The twenty-four hour mind: The role of sleep and dreaming in our emotional lives.* New York, NY: Oxford University Press.

Domhoff, G. W. (2011a). Dreams are embodied simulations that dramatize conception and concerns: The continuity hypothesis in empirical, theoretical and historical context. *International Journal of Dream Research*, 4(2), 50–62.

Domhoff, G. W. (2011b). The neural substrate for dreaming: Is it a subsystem of the default network? *Consciousness and Cognition*, 20(4), p. 1163–1174.

Flanagan, O. (2001). *Dreaming souls: Sleep, dreams, and the evolution of the conscious mind.* London: Oxford University Press.

Freud, S. (1900/2010). *The Interpretation of Dreams.* New York, NY: Basic Books.

Hartmann, E. (2011). *The nature and functions of dreaming.* New York, NY: Oxford University Press.

Kramer, M. (1991). The nightmare: A failure in dream function. *Dreaming*, 1(4), 277–285.

Kramer, M., & Glucksman, M. (2015). *Dream research: Contributions to clinical practice.* New York, NY: Routledge.

Malinowski, J. E. & Horton, C. L. (2015). Metaphor and hyperassociativity: The imagination mechanisms behind emotion assimilation in sleep and dreaming. *Frontiers in Psychology*, 6:1132.

McCarley, R. W., & Hobson, J. A. (1977). The neurobiological origins of psychoanalytic dream theory. *The American Journal of Psychiatry*, 134(11), 1211–1221.

Oaklander, M. (2015). The dream therapist. In *The Science of Sleep*, (pp. 42–45). New York, N.Y.: Time Inc. Books.

Olsen, M. R., Schredl, M., & Carlsson, I. (2013). Sharing dreams: Frequency, motivations, and relationship intimacy. *Dreaming*, 23(4), 245–255.

Rechstaffen, A., Bergmann, B., Everson, C., & Gilliland, M. (1989). Sleep deprivation in the rat: X. Integration and discussion of the findings. *Sleep*, 12(1), 68–87.

Revonsuo, A. (2000). The re-interpretation of dreams: An evolutionary account of the function of dreaming. Behavioral Brain Sciences, 23, 877–901.

Revonsuo, A., Tuominen, J. & Valli, K. (2015). The avatars in the machine: Dreaming as a simulation of social reality. In T. Metzinger & J. M. Windt (Eds). *Open MIND*: 32(T). Frankfurt am Main: MIND Group.

Schoch, S. F., Cordi, M. J., Schredl, M., & Rasch, B. (2018). The effect of dream report collection and dream incorporation on memory consolidation during sleep. *Journal of Sleep Research*, e12754. https://doi.org/10.1111/jsr.12754

Schredl, M. (2015). The continuity between waking and dreaming. In M. Kramer & M. Glucksman, (Eds.). *Dream research: contributions to clinical practice*, (pp. 27–37). New York, NY: Routledge.

Stickgold, R. (2002). EMDR: A putative neurobiological mechanism of action. Journal of Clinical Psychology, 58(1), 61–75.

Stickgold, R., Malia, A., Maguire, D., Roddenbury, D., & O'Connor, M. (2000). Replaying the game: Hypnagogic images in normal and amnesics. *Science*, 290, 350–353.

Valli, K., Revonsuo, A., Palkas, O., Ismail, K. H., Ali, K. J., & Punamäki, R. L. (2005). The threat simulation theory of dreaming: Evidence from dreams of traumatized children. *Consciousness and Cognition*, 14, 188–218.

Wamsley, E. J., Nguyen, N. D., Tucker, M. A., Olsen, A., & Stickgold, R. (2012). EEG correlates of overnight memory consolidation in a virtual navigation task. Sleep, 35, A86.

Wamsley, E. J., & Stickgold, R. (2010). Dreaming and offline memory processing. *Current Biology*, 20(23), R1010–R1013.

Wamsley, E. J., & Stickgold, R. (2011). Memory, sleep and dreaming: Experiencing consolidation. *Sleep Medicine Clinics*, 6(1), 97–108.

5 Understanding the Terrain
The Dream Is Born in Metaphor

A dream does not hide its message in metaphorical code. A dream is born metaphorically.
                                                                Eugene Gendlin

As the opening quote suggests, dreams do more than simply speak the language of metaphor, they *are* metaphor. As such, they speak a universal human language that predates or precedes the actual words we use, one that is based on embodied concepts we learn simply by living. Dreams and metaphor are fully embodied expressions that we then translate into language – and not the other way around. Understanding the dreamscape as expressed in metaphor helps us make sense of it, and to see that a dream is not the mind's attempt to obscure, but rather the body's attempt to communicate in the way that comes most naturally. Much of the strangeness and apparent obscurity of dreams is removed as soon as we understand that we should not take them literally but rather view them metaphorically.

The Physical Basis of Metaphor

The popular definition of metaphor is linguistic. Metaphor is often seen as a literary device where something concrete stands for something abstract: for example, a glass half-empty is a metaphor for pessimism, *cold feet* is a rather tired metaphor for wanting to back out of a commitment, and I was *touched (or moved)* by that poem uses a physical metaphor for an emotional response. What you will notice about all of these examples is that they have a physical basis, a familiar embodied experience as a way to express something more abstract. This was one of the major contributions of Lakoff and Johnson (1980/2003), whose classic book, *Metaphors We Live By* changed the way metaphor is conceptualized.

These ground-breaking ideas about metaphor have also met with resistance. *Metaphors We Live By* was published in 1980 and more than 20 years later, the authors noted several misconceptions about the nature of metaphor that persist. The first, alluded to above, is the idea that metaphor is merely a linguistic device. Second, that it is based on similarity of the two elements. They would say instead that metaphor is based on "cross-domain correlations" that bring new information. The other major misconceptions are related to how we conceptualize. Lakoff and Johnson build a convincing argument that the nature of human thought and reasoning originates in an embodied sense of the world and that all of our ideas and thought processes stem from that. A perfect example is found in the previous sentence: the use of the word "stem" is a metaphor, and the way a plant grows and forms new branches was used as a way to conceptualize the nature of thought processes.

I challenge you to convey *any* idea without the use of metaphor and I expect you will find that you simply can't do it. Again, in the previous sentence, there are at least three physical experiences standing in for concepts: challenge, convey and find. The major effect of Lakoff and Johnson's work was to bring our attention to the ubiquitous nature of metaphor, in particular those primary metaphors that we use to make sense of our world from the start. "There are hundreds of such primary conceptual metaphors, most of them learned unconsciously and automatically in childhood simply by functioning in the everyday world with a human body and brain." The authors state that we have no choice but to think and speak metaphorically since this mechanism is universal and automatic. Examples of primary metaphor derived from early embodied experience include: affection is warmth, important is big, down is bad, time is motion, and understanding is grasping (Lakoff & Johnson, 1999).

In his further writing specifically about dreams and metaphor, Lakoff (1993) concurred, concluding that "the system of conceptual metaphor plays a critical role in the interpretation of dreams. However, it cannot be used in isolation, without knowledge of the dreamer's everyday life to yield a meaningful interpretation." Lakoff makes what he calls a 'strong claim':

> The metaphor system plays a generative role in dreaming – mediating between the meaning of the dream to the dreamer and what is seen, heard, and otherwise experienced dynamically in the act of dreaming. Given a meaning to be expressed, the metaphor system provides a means of expressing it concretely – in ways that can be seen and heard. That is, the metaphor system, which is in place for waking thought and expression, is also available during sleep, and provides a natural mechanism for relating concrete images to abstract meanings.

The notion that metaphorical expression is available across waking thought and dreaming is not unique to Lakoff, but is worth noting. Many other forms of thinking fall away in dreaming, as we return to the more primal, embodied cognition and experiences we associate with metaphor. However, my sense is that dreams are far more than a particular way of *thinking* because they have a deeply experiential dimension and are dense, richly detailed and unexpected. What most people say about their dreams is that there is no way they could have thought of them, that they reflect a creativity beyond what the dreamer feels they possess.

Lakoff suggested that if Freud was right that dreams obscure their meaning, "the use of the conscious metaphor system in dreams is a perfect way for the unconscious mind to hide thoughts from the conscious mind while nonetheless thinking them." I tend to agree with those who believe dreams are not attempting to hide their meaning but to reveal it. Yes, dreams often express material that we repress (e.g. Malinowski, 2015). But I disagree that dreams are using metaphor as a way to hide our thoughts from ourselves. Rather, I think dreams are metaphorical because when we strip everything else away and return to the basic spatial-embodied language we all share as human beings (and even as animals), metaphor underlies it all.

Metaphor as a Vehicle for Emergent Meaning

Metaphor is not only a way to conceptualize and express our world, but also a way to create and express new ideas. The crossing of what are normally distant constructs stretches our imagination, and in this realm, dreams are a particularly rich source of novel and multi-faceted combinations. In dreams it becomes obvious that metaphor does not indicate similarity between the source and its target, but rather, it transfers meaning between them. According to Modell (2006), "By means of novel recombinations, metaphor can *transform* meaning and generate new perceptions. Imagination could not exist without this recombinatory metaphoric process." Modell goes on to describe how trauma degrades imagination and the metaphoric processes that update and recontextualize emotional memory. This results in the type of dreaming (and thought) characteristic of post-traumatic stress: concrete, frozen in time, and without imaginative capacity. Later, in the chapter on nightmares, I will provide an example of how dreamwork can rekindle impaired imagination.

Before we go on to consider how metaphor may be operating in some sample dreams, I will present a counterpoint to the view that dreams be considered metaphors for waking life, and the dream ego a representative of ourselves. Jenkins (2014) suggests that we should also take the dream at face value, on its own terms; it is not a metaphor until we translate it into a representation of waking life. "If we consider the dream from the perspective of the person who actually lives the dream, we discover a radically different view." Jenkins advocates for treating the dream itself as real, offering empathy for the dream ego's plight *within* the dream itself and for working with dreams in a way that improves life for the dream ego (quite apart from the ego of the dreamer). Jenkins suggests that translating the dream ego's plight into a waking life context marginalizes the dream world and abandons the dream ego. It is a form or prejudice against the actual experience of dreaming.

However, understanding dreams as metaphors for waking life underlies many forms of modern dreamwork. In the following examples, we will consider some examples of how metaphors can be understood and worked with in more typical dreams, with the understanding that here we are assuming these dreams are reflective of the dreamer's life situation. This reflects the philosophy of many but not all current clinical dreamwork methods.

Bear in the Kitchen Dream

A man dreams he is in a city apartment, and there is a mother bear in the kitchen who seems like she is about to attack. He throws a plate at her feet and she jumps straight up onto the top of the fridge as if lifted by an elevator. Then she leaves with her cub in tow.

In asking into associations to this dream, the dreamer relates it to his primary relationship, and notes that many of their conflicts are around household tasks, cooking in particular, so it makes sense to him that the dream takes place in the kitchen. At one point in working with the dream, I suggest he embody the bear. He feels the animal as a metaphor for his discomfort, and the things he says from the bear's perspective seem to depict his feelings well: *I am out of my element. I don't belong here. There is no ground to stand on. It is untenable for me to live here.* What he is saying feels true but before giving voice to his sense of the bear, he had not admitted to himself the depth of the desperation and dissatisfaction that was present. Dreams can bring what we repress right to the surface, and without the kind of softening and downplaying many of us will do with feelings we don't want to confront.

There is a considerable body of evidence to suggest the material in our dreams often reflects our most pressing current emotional concerns. Therefore, dreams like the one above, which is a metaphor for a primary relationship in conflict, are fairly common. There are even some typical metaphors, such as life as a journey, that lend themselves to visual and kinesthetic depictions of complex dynamics. What is important to understand about dream metaphors is that they are unique and particular to the dreamer. This bear in the kitchen means something to the man who dreamt it that would have a completely different meaning or make no sense at all to someone else.

According to one current theory of memory consolidation, our dreaming mind chooses very specific images from our life experience to visually and metaphorically represent information it deems important enough to consolidate for future use. According to Malinowski and Horton (2015), there are three key elements in dream metaphors: they provide a concrete image to represent an abstract concept, they refer to emotional events from waking life, and *it is necessary to discuss the image in detail with the dreamer* to grasp how it is a metaphor for an aspect of their life. Dream metaphors bring novelty because they loosely and creatively associate things that would not normally be put together. Tourangeau and Rips (1991) say metaphor leads to emergent meaning because it offers new ways to consider the relationship between seemingly-unrelated things. Malinowksi and Horton suggest that via dreaming we embody metaphors that enable us to assimilate current important emotional experience into our wider memory system and via dream metaphors, we also generate insight. In dreamwork, the process of exploring and making sense of our dream metaphors can enhance such insights by drawing our attention to implicit information thus making it more conscious. The word "insight" can itself be a metaphor for the process, as it describes the act of "seeing in."

According to Hartmann (2011), dreams are often composed of a central image that is a picture-metaphor for dreamer's current emotional landscape. His favorite example, because it is so direct and simple, is that of a tidal wave to depict the overwhelming wash of emotion following a major traumatic event. In a similar kind of example from my practice, a man dreamt there was huge fire sweeping towards his home, and he was going to have to evacuate. He was not particularly frightened in the dream, but in the brief time he had to gather his possessions, he felt compelled to take only his own paintings. In reflecting on this dream, he realized that in the midst of his current significant life changes, his creative pursuits were in danger of becoming a casualty. The dream showed him that he absolutely did not want that to happen. The conversation about his dream helped him re-align his priorities, an example of how dreamwork can lead naturally to the dreamer to insight that results in waking-life changes.

Many dreams contain not just one central image, but a series of connected images. Or they come in the form of a series of related images over time. For example, a woman dreamt of spiders off and on throughout her life, and could equate the times when spiders made their appearance as particularly stressful or challenging times, in particular those related to her lifelong deep conflicts with her mother. When she was a child, the spider dreams came with such intensity she would wake up in a panic and turn on the lights to make sure the spiders were not real. She said her life is now in a very good place, and the spider dreams are rare, but still occur when she is worried. Dreams like this can be diagnostic of a situation – for her they are a signal that something is wrong; they represent her fear or deep concern, and they feel dangerous and unexpected.

The Underwater Woman

The following dream series has a central metaphor that reflects the dreamer's long struggle with grief and loneliness following the loss of her husband of 30 years. *"Joan" dreamt that she was taking care of a young child for a strong, wise woman who lived in a house underwater in a cold, torrential current. It took all of Joan's strength just to hold the child and also hold on to something to anchor her. Surprisingly, she was not afraid and could tell she possessed the required strength... but just.*

This image of "just barely holding on" became an ongoing and powerful metaphor for her life situation. Joan expressed wonder that the woman whose child she was tending could live so easily in such a cold, inhospitable place. Yet when she sensed into herself in the dream, she found the surprising assurance that she could manage the situation. Over the course of our work together, the underwater woman revisited, both in subsequent dreams and in the visions that arose from her active imagination and meditation practice. Two months after the initial dream, she had a vision that the wise woman helped calm her lifelong fear of abandonment; when I asked her to revisit that, Joan could sense the woman's wide shoulders and strong arms in her own body. She said, "The wise woman is timeless, but the current changes. It isn't always so cold and relentless." A few months later, Joan said she was beginning to feel more like the wise woman than the one clinging for survival. In one of our sessions, she let her imagination take the image forward, climbed up a ladder to sit on a warm dock in the sun, and the child fell asleep on her lap.

The dream image appears to resolve itself, and we could simply leave it at that. Or we could consider the ways the dream parallels Joan's grief process, which moves from "barely hanging on" to embodying more of her strong, wise self and a sense of knowing she will be okay. She was severely neglected as a child, so the loss of her husband brought back deep-seated fears. She felt the child she was tending in the dream as a metaphor for her younger self, and the current as a metaphor for the changing flow of life. If viewed as a metaphor for the therapy relationship, I could be seen as the wise woman who is calming her down and lending my strength. I do not point to any of these metaphors in doing the dreamwork, but later I may engage in making connections with the dreamer wherever doing so seems to excite or energize her. In general, I may also tentatively inquire about any potential metaphoric connections that seem to be overlooked by the dreamer, fully prepared to drop that line of inquiry if it is not picked up.

As a final example, the following is a dream of mine that depicts a journey as metaphor for a life situation. Various types of journeys are common metaphors both in dreaming and in our everyday language for navigating relationships and the trajectory of our lives.

Runaway Jeep Dream

I'm riding in the front of a Jeep with a small dark man behind me driving. The controls are in the back seat. We're going very fast. The terrain is rugged, the road is curvy and undulating and it's very isolated. Suddenly, the man falls off the back and shouts to me to take the controls. It takes me a minute to realize the vehicle isn't going to stop, and that the accelerator is still on full speed ahead. I reach around behind me and find the steering wheel, but it feels awkward to steer from there. I need to get into the back seat, which is no easy feat in a speeding vehicle. I let go of the steering wheel to clamber over the seat, somehow knowing I won't go off the road. I jump in the back, keep driving, and am disappointed to find that I still can't find the brake. Eventually the vehicle slows and stops at the outskirts of a city and I get out and walk.

There is a lot of action in this dream, and the sense of moving too fast is something I can certainly relate to in my life. The dream also offers commentary on who is in control, and the precarious nature of that control. The sense of taking a back seat, and trying to steer from there is a complex, awkward, yet familiar feeling. The wild, runaway drive along the isolated road also feels like another apt metaphor for aspects of my life. There are many elements that might warrant further exploration such as: What does it mean to lose your guide? Or to drive from the back seat? What does getting out to walk imply? In working on this dream with a partner, I experientially re-enter the dream experience and find a surprising amount of joy in the wild ride that ensues.

Only the dreamer can say where the various inquiries will lead. I tend to favor experiential methods of dream explorations over intellectualizing, and this dream provides a good example of why this is the case. When I contemplated all of the interpretations I might give from just the dream text, many of them felt like lifeless platitudes such as: my life is moving too fast, I'm only sort of in control, and it's a rocky road. I can feel some of this as true, but there is nothing new in it for me. What makes me aware of the thrill of the experience is re-entry into the actual dream sensations; it was such a pleasant surprise.

As I write this, I have a sense there is more to understand about this dream. Sometimes dreams take time, and many sessions to open up – and I believe some dreams can be pondered for a lifetime. Some take patience and a few more life events to unfold before they make sense to us. There have been times when working with my own dream or a client's, that we were left with a sense that we didn't quite get what the dream was trying to say. I believe that given enough time and the right kind of attention, coming to some kind of understanding of the dream is always possible. Some dreams may be like works of art or novel experiences – meant to be marveled at or simply enjoyed rather than deciphered. I will discuss ways to categorize dreams next, but first I will offer an experiential interpretation of the runaway Jeep dream that may flesh out this complex personal metaphor.

The thing that puzzles me still is the notion of who is doing the driving. Who is the mysterious dark man that falls off the back of the Jeep? He's not someone I know, but a guide assigned to drive, and the only person who knows where we are going. Dream Interview questions might be useful here, a dreamwork method developed by Gayle Delaney (2016) as a reliable, methodical way to bridge the dream to waking life. This method is most famous for the device of asking the dreamer to explain each dream element as though she were from another planet. For example, the dreamworker could ask, "Imagine I'm from Mars. What is a Jeep? And what does it mean to steer it from the back seat?" To which I would answer, a Jeep is a utilitarian vehicle, good for navigating rough terrain. It seems I have the right vehicle for the job. But Jeeps are not meant to be steered from the back seat – the connotation is of a back seat driver, someone who calls the shots but is not actually doing the driving. They are always very annoying.

I think about the dark man who put the Jeep in fast motion toward our destination. I haven't got a sense of the purpose of the journey, don't know where we're headed, just that the road is remote, runs along a hilly, curvy ridge through rugged, mountainous terrain, mostly rock. We head out at full speed, going way too fast. Feeling the dream from inside my body, I can relate to the need to slow down. This is something I hear from everyone around me, but it's no less true for me. There seems to be no way to slow this ride down. What feels different to me from the inside versus the outside of the dream is how much fun it is, how exhilarating, like an amusement park ride, which I love. I am also feeling into how if I were to view this journey as a metaphor for my life situation, I would need to slow down, and start driving from the front seat. I can relate to this as well. I have a tendency to allow life to happen at times rather than setting an intentional direction. Possibly the dream is telling me I should be the driver of my own life rather than a passenger. When I consider that, it's not right. More accurately with respect to the dream, I am the driver but am not crystal clear about that, so I am making things much more difficult for myself than they need to be … .

I would carry on in this manner with the rest of the dream, but I already have a sense of gaining more personal insight than I had before engaging this line of inquiry. Simple, open-ended questions that presume nothing are effective ways to inquire into a dream. These are often meandering conversations that leave spaces for associations, and new memories from the dream to arise, as they often do when the dreamer is invited to flesh out their dream. The dream often returns to our mind's eye in rich sensory detail when we inquire into it in this manner. It never fails to astound me how very detailed and imaginative the dream world can be. As I imagine riding in the runaway Jeep, I can smell the chalky dust that the Jeep's tires kick up on the road. I can see the rugged black cloth upholstery in the Jeep's square, tiny back seat. It does seem crazy to try to drive from back there, especially on this road at this speed. As a further step, I might try embodying the dark man since he is the dream element that holds the information about where we are going and why.

From here, some dreamworkers love to ask more deeply into this question: How is this feeling similar your life experience right now? Or does this remind you of anything that happened yesterday? Part of me hates the question. My Jungian sensibilities rail against reducing the rocky wilderness of my dream world to a personal daytime concern. I can say it does feel like my life in some ways, in particular not being able to slow down, the madcap solo dash along the mountain ridge that is part scary, part fun. I can play with the metaphor until it's exhausted and see if I get the physical 'aha' response that tells me I've hit the mark. Taylor (1992) calls this "the only reliable touchstone of dream work." The dreamwork process is like the journey in my dream: an exploration with an unknown destination. But when we arrive, we will know it.

References

Delaney, G. (2016). Dream interview method. In J. E. Lewis & S. Krippner (Eds.). *Working with dreams and PTSD nightmares: 14 approaches for psychotherapists and counselors*. Santa Barbara, CA: Praeger.

Hartmann, E. (2011). *The nature and functions of dreaming*. New York, NY: Oxford University Press.

Jenkins, D. (2014). Not just another pretty metaphor: The ego's experience of dreaming. (Unpublished manuscript.)

Lakoff, G. (1993). How metaphor structures dreams: The theory of conceptual metaphor applied to dream analysis. *Dreaming*, 3(2), 77–98.

Lakoff, G. & Johnson, M. (1980/2003). *Metaphors we live by*. Chicago, IL: University of Chicago Press.

Lakoff, G. & Johnson, M. (1999). *Philosophy in the flesh*. New York, NY: Basic Books.

Malinowski, J. E. (2015). Dreaming and personality: Wake-dream continuity, thought suppression, and the Big Five Inventory. *Consciousness & Cognition*, 38, 9–15.

Malinowski, J. E., & Horton, C. L. (2015). Metaphor and hyperassociativity: The imagination mechanisms behind emotional assimilation in sleep and dreaming. *Frontiers in Psychology*, 6: 1132.

Modell, A. H. (2006). *Imagination and the meaningful brain*. Cambridge, MA: The MIT Press.

Taylor, J. (1992). *The wisdom of your dreams*. New York, NY: Jeremy P. Acher/Penguin.

Tourangeau, R., & Rips, L. (1991). Interpreting and evaluating metaphors. *Journal of Memory and Language*, 30(4), 452–472.

6 From Ordinary to Sublime
Kinds of Dreams

> *Significant dreams … are often remembered for a lifetime, and not infrequently prove to be the richest jewel in the treasure-house of psychic experience.*
>
> Carl Jung

A critical factor in deciding which is the best way to work with someone's dream is the type of dream they bring. You would work very differently with a harrowing nightmare than you would with an uplifting spiritual dream. Throughout history, there have been many systems developed to categorize dreams, many that predate the clinical use of dreams. People have been paying attention to their dreams since ancient times, and the understanding of the source and use of dreams varies widely depending on culture. A full description of the cultural history of dreaming is beyond the scope of this book. Kelly Bulkeley (2016) provides a good summary of the dreams from the Bible and from early philosophers (Aristotle, Artemidorus). Interestingly, a sense of the full array of opinions about the nature of dreams is represented in this sample, from dreams as messages from God (Bible), to dreams as meaningless (Aristotle), to dreams as relevant to personal waking life (Artemidorus). The debate about the nature of dreams continues into modern times, although those who believe dreams have no meaning are losing ground. In surveying the various kinds of dreams, I have surmised, as have many others before me, that there different dreams for different reasons across the night and across a lifetime.

This look at kinds of dreams is focused on Western culture starting in the 20th century. Jung (1945/1974) differentiated kinds of dreams specifically for clinical use. He drew a distinction between personal and transpersonal (collective) ways of knowing and suggested that the big dreams we sometimes experience are a reflection of the *archetypal* domain of the collective unconscious. These significant dreams are not to be read as purely personal commentary on the concerns of our daily lives, but to reflect the universal human experience. Jung wrote, "Not all dreams are of equal importance." He said that insignificant dreams

> are easily forgotten because their validity is restricted to the day-to-day fluctuations of the psychic balance. Significant dreams, on the other hand, are often remembered for a lifetime, and not infrequently prove to be the richest jewel in the treasure-house of psychic experience.

Jung differentiated dreams by their source: Everyday dreams are derived from our personal unconscious, while big dreams come from the collective unconscious and depict archetypal patterns shared by all human beings. It is at the archetypal level that Jung suggested one can look to the world's store of mythology and literature to amplify (flesh out, make sense of) the powerful images that live large in big dreams. There is yet another, higher level, Jung confusingly called the Self. These are the rare, numinous visitations via dreams by one's god-image, and they leave the dreamer awe-struck and in no need of interpretation.

Big Dreams

Big dreams can have such an impact on the dreamer that they can change the trajectory of their life. These dreams are considered so important, the International Association for the Study of Dreams (IASD) commissioned a project to gather a collection of big dream reports for the book *Dreams that change our lives* (Hoss & Gongloff, 2017). Hoss said such life-altering dreams may occur just once in a lifetime, and they seem to reflect an inner guiding wisdom that can function as a signpost for one's life. A dream can even save the dreamer's life. For example, a 54-year-old woman who contributed to the book had a dream the night before she had planned to commit suicide. In the dream, she is at the funeral of her best friend, and Jesus is standing at the back of the room angrily telling her that she has to deliver the eulogy. As she begins to speak, she finds she has to stop: "I feel the pain of every single person in that room all at one time." This brings her to the deeply-felt realization of how her own suicide would affect all of the people in her life, and it makes her change her mind about taking her own life. She wrote that although her suicidal feelings returned at times, from that day forward she knew she would never act on them.

This is one of numerous examples in the book of dreams that facilitate major life changes, including cancer recovery, choice of work or life partner, resolution of inner conflict, and spiritual transformation. When a client brings such a dream to therapy, especially one that has a clear and positive message, there is often little need for interpretation as the meaning is abundantly clear. Such dreams are best simply appreciated, their impact explored as much as the client wishes, and as often as they want. These dreams can be revisited over time, and their impact often endures. (See Chapter 13 for more on big dreams.)

Impactful Dreams

There are several kinds of dreams that have impact, and their effects differ, according to Don Kuiken who has made a comprehensive study of impactful dreams (Busink & Kuiken, 1996; Kuiken & Sikora, 1993). He defines impactful dreams as those that bring intense emotion that stays with us after awakening. The most familiar of such dreams is the *nightmare*, which leaves us shaken and frightened long after we wake up. Kuiken feels it is important to differentiate nightmares from the dream category he calls *existential* dreams because they should be treated differently in the process of psychotherapy. They are as unsettling as nightmares, but bring a qualitatively different sense that is not fear but "sublime disquietude." Kuiken (2015) says it would be a mistake to label such feelings as the typical kind of nightmare distress that clinicians work to dispel. Clients may be reluctant to let go of the deep feelings existential dreams bring because their magnitude "not only awakens [the dreamer] but also transports them to the limits of aesthetic expressibility."

The other kind of ineffable dream Kuiken and his colleagues have identified is the *transcendent* dream, which brings a distinctive feeling combination of ecstasy and awe and engenders feelings of power and competence in the dreamer. The final category, a catch-all for all of those dreams that are not impactful by Kuiken's definition, is *mundane* dreams. My sense is that these everyday dreams can be dismissed too easily, and after working with dreams for decades, I have come to the conclusion that there is no such thing as a mundane dream. Our more common dreams may not bring a deeply-felt and complex emotion that stays with us upon waking, and so are certainly in a different category than what Kuiken defines as impactful. But I have yet to find a dream that, once explored, had no impact on the dreamer. In fact, some of the smallest snippets of dreams, or exploration of elements that seem transparent and simple to interpret, have led to profound insights.

Dismissing a dream too soon is what Ullman (1996) called *dreamism*. He characterizes this as when

> the dreamer registers his dissatisfaction or even disdain for the dream by regarding it as too insignificant or too banal to bother with, or he thinks that its message is so obvious it is hardly worth the effort ... here is an irrational prejudice that in no way reflects the potential significance of the dream.

Ullman is best known for his development of a popular dream group protocol, and his conviction that we should appreciate rather than interpret dreams.

Lucid Dreams

Another category of dreams that warrants discussion is lucid dreaming, which is the experience of knowing you are in a dream while you are still dreaming, a sense of "waking up" within your dream. Such dreams can overlap with other categories – they can be nightmarish or transcendent for example – but they are also a unique phenomenon in their own right. Lucid dreaming has captured popular imagination as a result of films like *Inception* and *The Matrix*. It is also a helpful tool for dream researchers because it solves one of the major challenges of dream research: when we study dreaming, we have to rely on dreamer's reports after the fact, which may not accurately reflect the dreams themselves. When someone has the ability to become conscious while still dreaming, they can communicate directly from the dream state – although at this point what they communicate is limited to simple eye movements signaling they are conscious while dreaming.

It is much easier to recall dreams where some degree of lucidity is attained because there is a conscious mind present to record the dream material. Because of this and the fact that while lucid, dreamers have or can develop the ability to control some aspects of their dream experience, researchers and clinicians have been developing protocols to induce lucid dreaming and use this state as a form of therapy. The theory is that taking empowering action *within* the dream can translate into greater positive life change than imagining such action after the fact. Lucid dreaming has been shown to effectively treat trauma-related nightmares in this manner (e.g. Spoormaker & van den Bout, 2006). There is a large and increasing body of literature on lucid dreaming, well beyond the scope of this book. For our purposes, I will summarize the clinical use of lucid dreaming, briefly discuss the current research into how to induce lucid dreams and to what purpose, and will close with a brief clinical example.

Although lucid dreams did not begin to make their way into the clinical literature until the late-1980s, in fact such dreams are fairly common. About 50 percent of adults have experienced lucid dreaming, and about 20 percent experience lucid dreaming on a regular basis (Shredl & Erlacher, 2011). Lucid dreaming is also a skill that can be learned, although not by everyone, and not reliably. But our knowledge of how to induce lucid dreaming is increasing. In the lab, Michelle Carr and her colleagues (2018) were able to reliably induce *signal-verified* lucid dreaming in 54 percent of participants – meaning not only did they become lucid while dreaming, but also they were aware enough to move their eyes from back and forth four times, and this was clearly observable on the EEG trace recorded during their sleep lab nap sessions. Such a high success rate was possible because the researchers used pre-sleep training in which participants visualized becoming lucid in a dream in response to timed sound and light signals, and then, when the brainwaves of the person napping indicated they had entered REM sleep, the auditory and visual cues were replayed with the goal of triggering lucidity. Carr noted that four of the successful participants had never before experienced a lucid dream in their life, suggesting this protocol works even with inexperienced lucid dreamers.

Those without the benefit of sleep lab technology are less successful at having lucid dreams on any consistent basis. But for dedicated would-be lucid dreamers, there are techniques available that increase the likelihood of success. For example, lucid dream pioneer and expert Stephen LaBerge and colleagues (1995) have developed a technique called mnemonic induction of lucid dreaming (MILD) to increase a person's chances of lucid dreaming. The technique includes setting a vividly imagined intention to have a lucid dream, and engaging in reality testing during the day by asking oneself periodically, am I dreaming? Waking up earlier than usual and spending 30 to 60 minutes meditating and/or focusing on reentering a dream before going back to sleep has been shown to help induce lucid dreams as well (Levitan & LaBerge, 1989). More recently, LeBerge and colleagues (2018) studied adding specific doses of a substance called galantamine to the protocol, and this was found to not only significantly increase dream lucidity, but also recall, clarity, control, vividness and positive emotion in the resulting dreams. So, for the motivated dreamer, there are ways to acquire and develop skills in lucid dreaming, and to carry these much further in the far realms of dreaming experience.

However, this takes us beyond the scope of this book. For most dreamworkers not specifically focused on lucidity, this added dimension is welcome, but does not dramatically change how one works with the dream. For those interested in exploring this realm further, there is a wealth of literature on the topic.

Kinds of Disturbing Dreams: Nightmares, Night Terrors and Sleep Paralysis

The most common form of bad dream is the nightmare, which researchers usually define as a disturbing dream that wakes the dreamer up. Most often, nightmares are frightening, although intense sadness or any other harrowing emotion can feature in a nightmare. Because there are many special considerations in working with nightmares clinically, the topic is covered in its own chapter later in the book. Here I will outline other forms of disturbed dreaming that sometimes get mistaken for nightmares.

Night terrors are short intense episodes in which the dreamer may cry out in their sleep and appear to be experiencing extreme fear. However, upon waking, those who have night terrors will have no recollection of the episode or of dreaming. It is fairly easy to differentiate night terrors from nightmares – they are most often experienced by children, they take place early in the course of a night's sleep, and they are not recalled upon waking despite how terrified the dreamer appears to an observer.

Sleep paralysis is another sleep disturbance that people sometimes associate with nightmares. During REM sleep and dreaming, our brain releases a chemical that paralyzes us from the neck down to keep us safe from acting out our dreams. Sometimes people wake up before the paralysis has lifted, creating the terrifying feeling in the dreamer that they are awake but trapped in their own body. Those who experience sleep paralysis often report the sensation of a heavy weight on their chest and the sense of a presence in the bedroom with them. In Newfoundland, sleep paralysis is so common, there is a name for it, a visit from the "old hag" (Firestone, 1985). This phenomenon occurs in about one-third of the population and is more common during periods of sleep deprivation and stress.

Precognitive Dreams

There are multiple ways in which dreams can have a purchase on the future, and precognitive or prophetic dreams can be located within this broader category. According to kitt price, a researcher and lecturer at Queen Mary University who is writing a cultural history of precognitive dreams, predictive dreams can operate at the somatic level and relay information about the course of disease, and they can operate in the psychological domain, helping the dreamer solve problems or prepare for life events.

> This can be literal, for instance when rehearsing a task in a dream prior to repeating it in waking life, or it can be symbolic, where dream preparation for subsequent waking activity either functions subconsciously, or emerges through a process of dream work.

The preparative function of dreaming shades into the precognitive when scenes from a dream are repeated verbatim in subsequent waking life, or when action taken on the basis of dream content changes the course of waking events (for example when a person intervenes to prevent an accident, or profits in some material way on the basis of dream information). Price said that in the 1960s, prophetic dreams were taken seriously: the British Bureau of Premonitions, and the Central Premonitions Bureau in New York were established to coordinate dream information from the masses with the goal of preventing disasters. Many precognitive dreams are quite trivial, however, relating to less dramatic events from the dreamer's future.

K. price (January 2019, personal communication) has found that precognitive dreamers can be reluctant to disclose their experience to others for fear of being judged as mentally ill.

> The experience of having dream content replay in subsequent waking life can be disorienting and unsettling; it can be experienced positively or negatively depending on a range of factors such as transpersonal beliefs and whether the dreamer has a community in which dreams are valued. It's worth remembering that dreams may not operate with the same temporality as waking life, and that the divisions we make into past, present and future may not consistently apply to dream content.

Price suggests that when a dream does spontaneously connect with subsequent events in waking life, it's best to keep an open mind.

Recurrent Dreams and Dream Series

Another dream phenomenon to be aware of is the recurring dream. There are many versions of this dream, but the most famous is of course, the recurring trauma nightmare, which is the hallmark symptom of PTSD. What characterizes PTSD nightmares, and sets them apart is that they tend to replicate a traumatic real-life incident, and very little changes from dream to dream, even over long stretches of time. More typical recurring dreams have slight changes, or major ones over time that can be seen as reflective of changes in the dreamer's mental health, attitude or life situation. In general, recurring dreams are negatively-toned, take place more often in times of stress, and reflect disruption or lack of resolution in the life of the dreamer. They are to be distinguished from recurring dream themes that more generally stay with a person throughout their life and do not indicate trouble (Bonime, 1962).

It is possible to track clinical progress by the evolving nature of a person's recurring dreams. Zadra (1996) surveyed numerous studies on recurring dreams and consistently found that the cessation of a recurrent dream is associated with increased levels of well-being in adults. "These findings underscore the importance of examining series of dreams instead of focusing solely on individual dreams."

One way to track change over a series of dreams is to pay attention to how the "I" or dream-ego in the dream evolves. In nightmare research, when the dreamer is encouraged to change their dream, it is often the increased mastery on the part of the "I" in the dream that appears to lead to an improved dream life. An advocate for the dream ego, Jenkins (2014) believes these dream characters get short shrift when they are seen as merely an avatar of the dreamer. Their plight is often harrowing and dramatic, yet attention is rarely turned toward their feelings or toward helping them in their predicament. Jenkins feels dream therapy is best directed toward improving dream life itself, rather than only focusing on how it relates directly to the dreamer's waking life.

Scott Sparrow's (2013) FiveStar method of dreamwork is an exception in this regard because attending to the dream ego's experience is in fact a central part of the process. In FiveStar, emphasis is placed on the interactions within the dream between the dream ego and the autonomous aspects of the dream. Sparrow highlights the co-creative nature of dreams, specifically how the dream ego and dream interact to create the dream narrative. This points to the experience we have all had in dreams when something devastating is about to happen, and through force of our own will and/or some action on the part of the "I" in the dream, the scene shifts in a way that saves the night. FiveStar links dream ego to dreamer and suggests changes in the way the dreamer's avatar acts in the dream world may help shift the dreamer out of chronic, unhelpful waking life patterns.

As recurring dream series develop over time, many things can change in addition to the characteristics of the dream ego. For example, dreams of those with depression tend to have more aggressive and fewer friendly interactions than do those of a non-depressed person (Domhoff, 2015), so a sustained positive shift in a dream's social landscape can be seen to predict, or coincide with a lifting of depression. Dream unfriendliness is also higher in more severe psychopathology such as schizophrenia and psychosis. The prevailing mood or style of a person's dreams can evolve over time, and reflect what we as clinicians often hope for our clients: change. In general, people's dreams cover the same themes over a lifetime, so any significant lasting change in the dream landscape can be seen as marking change in the dreamer, ideally for the better.

References

Bonime, W. (1962). *The clinical uses of dreams*. New York, NY: Basic Books.
Bulkeley, K. (2016). *Big dreams: The science of dreaming and the origins of religion*. London: Oxford University Press.
Businck, R., & Kuiken, D. (1996). Identifying types of impactful dreams: A replication. *Dreaming*, 6(2), 97–119.
Carr, M., Konkoly, K., Mallett, R., Edwards, C., Appel, K., & Blagrove, M. (2018). A technique for inducing high levels of signal-verified lucid dreams in a laboratory morning nap. *Journal of Sleep Research*, 27.
Domhoff, G. W. (2015). Friends and friendliness: Could they be the clue in psychiatric patients' dreams? In M. Kramer & M. Glucksman, (Eds.). *Dream research: Contributions to clinical practice*, 67–79. New York, NY: Routledge.
Firestone, M. (1985). The "old hag" sleep paralysis in Newfoundland. *Journal of Psychoanalytic Anthropology*, 8(1), 47–66.
Hoss, R. J. & Gongloff, R. P., Eds. (2017). *Dreams that change our lives*. Asheville, NC: Chiron Publications.
Jenkins, D. (2014). Not just another pretty metaphor: The ego's experience of dreaming. (Unpublished manuscript.)
Jung, C. G. (1945/1974). Dreams. In *Collected Works of C.G. Jung*, Bollingen Series XX. Princeton, NJ: Princeton University Press.
Kuiken, D. (2015). The contrasting effects of nightmares, existential dreams and transcendent dreams. In M. Kramer & M. Glucksman (Eds.). *Dream research: Contributions to clinical practice*. New York, NY: Routledge.
Kuiken, D., & Sikora, S. (1993). The impact of dreams on waking thoughts and feelings. In A. Moffitt, M. Kramer, and R. Hoffman (Eds.). *The functions of dreaming*, (pp. 419–476). Albany, NY: State University of New York Press.
LaBerge, S., & Levitan, L. (1995). Validity established of DreamLight cues for eliciting lucid dreaming. *Dreaming*, 5(3), 159–168.
LaBerge, S., LaMarca, K., & Baird, B. (2018). Pre-sleep treatment with galantamine stimulates lucid dreaming: A double-blind, placebo-controlled, crossover study. *PLoS ONE*, 13(8), e0201246.
Levitan, L. & LaBerge, S. (1989). A comparison of three methods of lucid dream induction. *Nightlight*, 1(3), 3–12.
Sparrow, G. S. (2013). A new method of dream analysis congruent with contemporary counselling approaches. *International Journal of Dream Research*, 6(1), 45–53).
Spoormaker, V. I. & van den Bout, J. (2006). Lucid dreaming treatment for nightmares: a pilot study. *Psychotherapy and Psychosomatics*, 75(6), 389–394.
Ullman, M. (1996). *Appreciating dreams: A group approach*. New York, NY: Cosimo-on-Demand.
Zadra, A. (1996). Recurrent dreams: Their relations to life events and well-being. In Barrett, D., (Ed.). *Trauma and dreams*. Cambridge, MA: Harvard University Press.

7 Navigating the Dream Divide
Woman in the Mirror Dream

All life is only a set of pictures in the brain, among which there is no difference betwixt those born of real things and those born of inward dreamings, and no cause to value the one above the other.
H. P. Lovecraft

Common factors research indicates that today's dreamworkers have much more in common than we have differences. There is a distinct trend toward greater experiential exploration of dreams and away from interpretation. However, there remains a philosophical divide about the essential direction and purpose of dreamwork, which reflects polarized beliefs about the nature of dreams. Some dreamworkers make the connection of dreams to waking life situations central to their method, while others suggest we avoid this at all costs in favor of an interactive experience with the dream itself. This chapter first offers an explanation of the "dream divide" in terms of neuroscience, and then uses some selections from the menu of "common factors" choices to provide a detailed example of the avenues used in a focusing-oriented dreamwork session, which falls on the dream-centric (vs. self-centric) side of the dream divide.

Most people with whom I have discussed this will tell me there is no definitive answer, or that the dream can be both/and: personal and/or transpersonal, and many gradations besides. That feels true, but it can lead to a sense that anything goes and result in dream exploration that becomes an indistinct mix of methods. This may not be a problem either, as dreams respond well to meandering curiosity. But I have a sense of each dream as an opportunity, a gift that can only be opened for the first time once. Gendlin (2012) said this about this nature of process: if you start with a raw egg, you have many options, but once you boil it, you can no longer fry it. If a dream is like a raw egg, then what you do with it first in terms of cooking it, matters and affects what you can and can't do with it next. I believe there is inherent power in the initial exploration of a dream. Therefore, as a dreamworker, it is important to decide which path you're taking with the dream, and then to be conscious of speaking about the dream in those terms. At times you or the client may switch gears from a personal to a more cosmic perspective or vice versa, much in the same way that a dream can abruptly shift scenes. If you keep tabs on the movement of perspective, you can change your language and line of inquiry accordingly to keep the dreamer in the experiential flow. This may sound complicated, but in fact, much of this will happen automatically in the flow of dream dialogue.

We still have the question: which path to take first? I consider both the nature of the dream and developmental process of the dreamer. I often start with a general question about their impressions of the dream and invite an experiential re-telling to see what comments or new images might drop into the narrative. All of these are clues about how best to enter the dream dialogue. With respect to the dream itself, sometimes the waking life connection appears to be a clear key to the dream, and at other times as though reducing it to a personal issue would diminish or disrespect the dream. Of course every dream can have layers, some with personal and some with larger significance and beginning in once place does not preclude visiting another. Still, it feels important to consider where you are and how you navigate the "dream divide" right from the very start of your mutual encounter with the dream.

The "Dream Divide"

In working toward a universal dreamwork method, I have repeatedly encountered many versions of the same philosophical divide: the question of whether and how much to relate our dreams to our waking life concerns. That at least some portion of our dreams is about our waking life has been established by dream researchers, however this accounts for only a small proportion of our dream content, no more than 20 percent. Tying dream images back to our lives via the process of association is almost a ubiquitous dreamwork method, but the reason for doing so varies considerably. Some methods, such as Bosnak's embodied imagination, ask for associations simply to bracket them out so the dreamer can participate more fully in the what he aptly calls the "wilderness" of their dream world. Other methods, such as Delaney's dream interview technique or the Ullman dream group process, make connecting dream images with waking life concerns central to the process.

As we just saw in the chapter on metaphor, sometimes our entire dream image might be seen as one long extended metaphor for the particular emotional situation we find ourselves in during waking life. Making this connection can bring enormous, and deeply-felt insight. However, we can also be impacted by the dream experience without making such a direct connection to our life by simply allowing the dream experience to fill us up. This has the experiential energy to evoke change in us, and after such a shift, the implications related to waking life often filter in naturally over the ensuing days or weeks.

The Divide as a Function of Our Bilateral Brain

One way to consider the main philosophical divide in dreamwork is as different ways of seeing depending on which cerebral hemisphere is mediating our perspective. Part of the reason dreamwork has been shuffled to the sidelines of mainstream psychotherapy is that there are "left-shifted" biases being built into our profession. The emphasis on evidence-based practices, repeatable protocols, symptom reduction and outcome measures all stem from an orientation mediated by the left side of our brain which craves facts and certainty (Badenoch, 2018).

These ideas about how differently we see the world based on whether our right or left hemisphere is dominant is the main premise in *The Master and his Emissary*. In this highly-influential book based on a decade of research, McGilchrist (2009) carefully documents the differences in ways of relating to the world depending on whether our experience is being mediated more by the right or left hemisphere. Any summary of brain function will be both a gross oversimplification and a misunderstanding of the actual process because our research into brain function is still quite primitive. That said, Badenoch (2018) offers a simple way to tell when we are left-shifted in our approach, and notes that about 75% of us in Western society approach the world in this way. It is often a desire for certainty that prompts this left shift, and a step away from feeling too deeply, using the intellect as a defense against emotion. You can tell you are in this mode when you begin to use machine metaphors for the ways people behave. For example, in therapy, the left-shift reveals itself in our desire to diagnose and repair, which uses a machine analogy for the human psyche.

Right-shifted language is inclusive, present-focused, open-ended and concerned with nuance and particularity. This way of approaching the world is relational and phenomenological, and differs from the goal directed left-shifted tendency to value only those things that can be put to our personal use. It is tempting then to view right-hemisphere values as superior, but that itself is, ironically, a left-shifted view of things. Ideally, we operate with both hemispheres in relationship with each other, but with the right as the master, and the left as the emissary, as McGilchrist's book title suggests.

In the context of dreamwork, what I believe this suggests is that a whole-brain approach would be open-ended, attuned to individual experience and yet informed by science and the therapeutic goals of the client. I also believe that dreamwork itself is more of a right-shifted endeavor, dreams being unique, mysterious and operating outside of linear daytime logic. This is supported by a brain imaging study (Benedetti, 2015) that showed differences in the activation of specific, mainly right-brain areas (right inferior frontal gyrus, right superior and middle temporal gyrus) when a person recalls a dream they actually experienced versus a dream they read or listened to while awake. It appears there is something unique (and right-shifted) that happens when we recall our own dreams. As such, working with dreams might have the effect of bringing our left-shifted way of being more into balance.

Expanding Perspectives: More Ways to Consider Dreams

To expand one's perspective on the purpose of dreamwork, it is useful to consider how other cultures attend to and make use of their dreams. Ancient and indigenous cultures tend to have a more communal, 'right-shifted' and engaged relationship with their dreams compared with Western society. These *polyphasic* cultures, which are differentiated by Laughlin and Rock (2014) from modern, materialistic *monophasic* culture, tend to share a set of beliefs about dreaming that stands in stark contrast to the modern viewpoint. Polyphasic cultures have a deep relationship to their dreams, tend to view them as real not imaginary, and communal rather than personal. In fact Laughlin's research (2013) suggests there are more people in this world who view dreams as a form of reality than do not. And as Lovecraft's opening quote suggests, there may be no reason to value the 'real' world over the dream world.

Another inclusive way to consider dreams is as if they represent a developmental process (e.g. Siegel, 2016). When we first begin to consider our dreams, they often represent a personal perspective reflective of the more egocentric stages of early development. As we go about the business of life, navigating work and personal relationships, our dreams often reflect these concerns. If we attend to our dreams during times when we are deeply and busily engaged with life, they often both reflect this and help us by bringing fresh perspectives. When we turn toward the end of life, or face major illness or existential crises, dreams can also meet us there and ease our passage through difficult times, and major transitions.

Yet another way to enlarge one's perspective on the possible ways to approach a dream is to consider their many layers of meaning, and the possibility that what they are bringing may take time and attention to fully realize. For example, in the dreamwork session below, the dreamer was content to experience the dream itself, making minimal associations to waking-life, and mostly staying with the striking dream image; it seemed to offer something about the nature of her dream world, and maybe of dreaming itself. Only later, and because she referred back to the dream on subsequent days, did she feel its connection to something significant from her past, and it was helpful on that level as well.

70 *Navigating the Dream Divide*

So as you go through the dreamwork decision tree, you might consider all of this – your own philosophical understanding of dreams, the kind of dream the dreamer brings, their point of view about the dream, and where they are in their life. As you guide the dreamer back into the dreamscape, you can get a feel for where the dreamer may want to take it, which side of the divide.

The Dreamwork Decision Tree

All methods begin with a telling of the dream, and from there, next steps can vary considerably, and for many reasons. Below, I present a clinical example and show in bold which steps were followed in this case from the menu of "common factors" dreamwork techniques I introduced in Chapter 3, as well as brief commentary on my choice of methods. I hope to illustrate that working with dreams is not formulaic, but more of a mutual exploration following not only your theoretical orientation, but also your curiosity and in-the-moment responses to the interaction between the dreamer and their dream. You can see that this example is not one where the dreamworker directly pursued waking life connections and specific insight or growth steps within the session itself. As it turned out, staying close to the dream itself was a strong preference on the part of the dreamer. Insight and connections to her life came spontaneously to the dreamer a few days after the session but only because I asked about the dream again, so I have added it here as a step.

> **Tell the dream** (Ideally, as it was done here, in first-person, present tense.)
> **Explore the setting, including the emotional landscape**
> **Ask into associations** (This was very brief, not so much a focus of the session.)
> **Experiential exploration of dream elements** (Being a dream element, dreaming it onward.)
> **Explore metaphorical and other connections to waking life** (Very limited in this session)
> Name and explore new insights and growth steps (This happened later.)

Optional avenues

> Amplification using symbol or myth
> Art or creative expression
> Reformulation to generic terms
> Compensation (Not pursued, but this shift does happen in this case example.)
> Story or plot structure
> **Finding help in the dream** (Yes, after many tries.)
> Pursuing/exploring lucidity (This was a possible avenue, but not taken here.)
> **Allowing the dream to continue** (Allowing the dream its autonomy was key.)
> Group projections onto the dream
> Action step, life change, new creation or direction
> **Follow up** (Brought insight and connections to waking life)

Woman in the Mirror Dream

In this extended clinical example, the actual dialogue between the dream therapist and dreamer is provided, with some editing for sake of brevity. To begin, the dreamer is asked to tell her dream, and does so naturally in an experiential mode, using first-person, and present tense.

I "come to" in this dream and I have this vague understanding that I was at a party the previous night and had no recollection of what had happened. I am very disoriented and confused. I go into the bathroom. One of the walls is a mirror, the whole wall is just a mirror, and I'm looking at myself in the mirror. I can see my reflection but it's kind of off to the side and a bit distant. It is a woman wearing a white dress. I start talking and realize she is not talking at the same time – she is moving her head and looking at different times than me, so I realize I'm dreaming because of that. I tell the reflection that this is a dream and she seems a bit angry at me for that. Other reflections appear, several versions of me all moving at slightly different times from me and the whole scene is very creepy. I tell all of them in the mirror, it's okay, it's a dream, you can do what you want to, you can have fun. And at the same time, I am trying to calm myself down, trying to focus on my breathing. I don't want to be nervous because it's just a dream. After that the whole dream starts to fade away. The whole room and the people in the mirror just disappear and the dream ends with me still kind of lucid. I can hear my breathing and at some point I just wake up.

THERAPIST: We're going to explore the setting in the dream. Can you visualize it and explore it a bit?

CLIENT: I'm in a room that was supposed to be a bathroom, but it just consists of the whole wall in front of me that is a mirror. I can just feel I'm in a closed room. My reflection is a bit distant, is moved back so I can see the whole shape of a woman in a long white, wedding-like dress. That's the main setting, me in a room looking at this woman in the mirror.

T: The woman in the mirror, does she look exactly like you?

C: No not exactly, but I also don't really know what I am supposed to look like. It seems like it is me but a different version of me. I don't have a sense of what I'm wearing, but she has brown hair and a long white dress that's a bit tattered.

T: Does the reflection look like anybody else you know?

C: More like me than anyone else, but the color my hair used to be I guess.

T: Is it a past you or just different?

C: I guess it's a bit past. Even when I'm looking at her face, I can't really picture what she looks like.

T: Do you get any kind of a sense from her, like how she's feeling or…?

C: I feel kind of anxious anticipating something, it's kind of a negative scene, she has horror movie creepy vibes.

T: You start talking and she's talking but not at the same time.

C: I think I noticed something felt off, so I started moving my mouth and moving my head and then realizing that her mouth and her head were moving at slightly different times.

T: And how did that feel?
C: More creepy. I think I realized I was dreaming at that point. It also gave the scene in the mirror more power because it had its own life. I wasn't just looking in a mirror, there was something going on back there.
T: Did you have any sense of what you thought might be going on?
C: Not really. It made me anxious because it seems like something not so great was happening back there.
T: Did you just stay in the same place, or did you move?
C: I realized I was dreaming so I said something like, 'This is a dream.' I started looking at other areas of the mirror. More scenery appeared, and more people, more versions of me, all moving at slightly different times, so creepy. I felt like she didn't appreciate my saying it was a dream and that's when more people appeared, and they equally did not seem like the most happy-go-lucky characters. They all seemed displeased with me.
T: They were displeased that you were saying it was a dream?
C: I think they were displeased with me generally. They all seemed like they were trapped in a way. They were all on one side of this and I was on the other side saying it's just a dream.
T: So you felt like they were trapped.
C: Maybe trapped isn't the right word, but they were all part of a different reality or something, a different story.
T: I wanted to ask about the characters – are they all wearing the same white dress?
C: No they're all different, wearing different things and they all look slightly different. I think they all have the same body type and posture and face though it's not that clear, just slightly different styles of clothing and hair.
T: And in this part, is the you, the woman in the white dress, is she still the clearest in the reflection?
C: Yes.
T: Are there any associations that you make in your waking life to that dress?
C: Only the simple association that I was watching an episode of *Friends* and they are all wearing wedding dresses.
T: I think you said the wedding dress was slightly tatty.
C: It was kind of torn. I can't see too clearly. The whole scene back there was grungy and torn, and dark and dreary and sad.
T: So I wonder if you can maybe try to feel into the woman in the white dress. (This prompting to enter into the dream element, to become the woman, is familiar to the dreamer, so could be offered in this succinct way. Such brief instruction may not work with all dreamers.)
C: Ok… (pause). I can imagine seeing me walk into the room, it just feels like the me in the bathroom is looking through a cage at the zoo, and I'm just like on display or something. It's got a graveyard feel to it.
T: So behind the mirror there's a graveyard feel.
C: It also feels like she can't really see me, the person in the bathroom who is looking through this glass in this nice bathroom… it doesn't feel like she can really see me.

T: But she knows you're there?
C: It's almost like she… it's like the me in the bathroom can see the woman, but is not really paying attention, or doesn't care or notice me (as the white-dress woman).
T: And so if you are embodying the woman in the dress, do you sense what she feels toward you?
C: Yes, it's like an aching, wanting to be seen or like, she seems really sad. She is wanting my attention. It's like the me in the bathroom can see the scene but doesn't think of it as real. The bathroom feels like the real place, whereas the woman wants me to see that her situation is real too, or to see and connect with her. She feels lonely.
T: So the woman seems like she is part of a different reality, but for her, she wants you to recognize that she's real?
C: To me in the bathroom it's not real, it's just like a scene. And even when I'm lucid I think, that's just a dream. Whereas to the woman in the white dress, the bathroom is what seems like a façade.
T: Because the dream is asking for connection, my impulse is to ask, is there any way you can give her what she's asking for? To treat her with more seriousness or to cross over… or is there a way to connect with her? And I wouldn't try to presume what that might be, but is there a way to give her what she's asking for?
C: I will go into it imaginatively… (long pause)… I can try, but they seem so separate.
T: So maybe if that feels like too much of a stretch, you might try it from the reverse, to be her and see if she can reach across. It seems like the mirror has become a sort of barrier in a way.
C: (long pause)… it seems like from this perspective that, it's hard to describe, it seems like there's a whole world back here. And the bathroom seems like a little viewing room into this world. I still can't cross the barrier but it has changed – like the me in the bathroom is in a little viewing room.
T: It's like from her perspective you're the one in the smaller world.
C: Yeah because at the beginning I was looking into this one little scene and everything from my side of the mirror seemed like the real world, whereas now it seems like I'm in this little viewing room and on the other side is this big world with lots of versions of me and of experiences and things that are all on the other side.
T: Interesting, so do you see anything more when you look around there?
C: I can't see things that clearly, it's like a huge space with tons of scenes. This woman in the white dress in the graveyard is just one scene and there are a bajillion different ones back there. I said the woman is lonely but more just wanting to be seen I guess. It seems much bigger than when I started actually. It has completely changed my understanding of what's going on back there.
T: How would you articulate that, how it's changed?
C: Just like the centre of the dream has changed. Before it was me and everything behind the mirror seemed ephemeral and blurry and not very concrete, whereas now even though I can't describe things that clearly, it feels very real

back there and it feels like there are so many different versions of me, and so many different places even though I can't see them.

T: It sounds like very much a description of what the dream world could be like, many versions and trying to reach you. What I wonder, now that this has changed so much, is if you could go back to looking through the mirror to see if that's changed too?

C: (long pause)… The main difference is, I think I said the word creepy five times because I was anxious about what was going on back there. Now I don't feel anxious and it's not creepy. It's still a bit sad but I don't feel scared… it still seems like the woman is sad.

T: Is it still about not being able to connect or reach you somehow or…?

C: It's something like that. A lack of connection. There is just some barrier between us.

T: Now that you've gotten a bit further into it, can you see if there is some way for you to connect with that woman and her world? That's what the dream seems to be asking for.

C: (long pause) I haven't gotten too much further. It seems a bit better, and… they still seem so separated.

T: Let me read back to you what I've heard. You're looking through a mirror and your dream figure in the mirror is asking you for connection and to be taken seriously. She's saying something like, I am not just a figment of your imagination, there's much more to this. Is that something that lands for you, that your dreams are saying, hey there's a lot more here than you are giving us credit for or something like that? (This is a plot summary technique, which can illuminate the dream story for the dreamer.)

C: My initial experience was slightly anxious. I tried to ignore it in a way because I didn't want to be scared. Whereas the dream doesn't like that. It is a common feeling, something I experience often in dreams, I start to feel nervous about something. It's the unpredictable, wild nature of dreams that makes me nervous so I try to downplay and ignore it but that doesn't really help. There is definitely a message that's recurring and resonates with me but there still seems to be some block. The need is to not be anxious about it, but I don't know how to do that.

T: So can you feel the anxiety that was in the dream. I notice you are actually calming yourself down during the dream, can you get a felt sense of that… from the dream, and where it lives in you just in general? (This is a focusing-specific section, asking into the bodily-felt sense.)

C: It's like a big anxiety in my stomach and my mind saying, just look away.

T: Can you sit with that feeling in your stomach and be curious, try to be welcoming, and describe what you're sensing as much as you can?

C: It just feels like lots of rumbling and jitteriness in my whole abdomen. It takes up all the space in my stomach and pressing up against the sides of my body.

T: Wow, it's big. Is this really familiar?

C: Definitely.

T: If you ask into that big fear, ask what it's afraid of?

C: (pause) I don't get a clear response… I don't know…

T: What happens when you do that, it stays the same? Doesn't give you much?

C: The sense is very clear but I don't get any response from it.

T: What about checking to see what would help. I guess it's already somewhat told you it's the fear of the unpredictability and going into that, so you ignore it… so just ask it right from this discomfort in your belly. Because I think of discomfort as at least partly meaning your body wants something different and there's a way forward. So if you could ask it what would be the way forward, maybe it could show you in terms of your dream image… or really be open to however it might show you because it could come in many forms.

C: Ok it's weird. I'm back in the dream and the first thing is going up to the glass and putting my hands and my face fully pressed into it, and it kind of becomes a bit liquidy. I just go into the glass halfway and that's where I should be. I'm not supposed to go all the way into that world. It seems like tons of versions of me and my experiences. I need to be completely in the barrier. It's not supposed to disappear, I'm supposed to just be in it. Be one with the barrier so I have myself on both sides. I'm not supposed to completely enter it, just approach it completely.

T: What's it like when you do that?

C: It makes my body feel like I am the barrier, extended. Before it seemed like a viewing window into this whole world, whereas now because I am the glass, I can see all of the world. I am just present with all of it.

T: Wow, that's wild… So what does that do in your stomach?

C: I still have that feeling, but normally I just avoid it. Whereas if it happens and I'm in the glass, it's still there, and I can't move or anything, am completely spread open and stuck there but it doesn't feel like a negative thing. It feels like I am totally in it, totally in that sense of my stomach, that grumbling, pulsing, I'm just totally in it.

T: So not avoiding, that's different.

C: Yeah completely.

T: So I'm wondering if you could try one more thing. With you completely in the glass and not avoiding, can you go back to the woman in the white dress just to see what that's like from her perspective?

C: She's just very relieved. And really grateful. (The wave of feeling is visible in the client's face, and tears come.)

T: So just stay there for a little bit. Feel the relief and the gratitude.

C: At first it was super overwhelming gratitude.

T: What does that do to your body when you feel all that?

C: It feels a bit like releasing some tension, or a bit like a spreading of the sensations I was feeling earlier.

T: Because it sounds like it feels pretty good, just stay there for another minute, just feeling the spreading, the relief.

C: It feels like I guess maybe from the perspective of the woman in the white dress it feels like someone watching over you. (The session begins to feel softer, almost sacred.)

T: Nice. Does that feel like a good place to stop, or does it feel like anything more needs to happen?

C: No it feels good. That was a long and complicated case huh?

T: I don't know if you can ever really predict these things, but it took a long time to find the place in the dream that feels good. Basically until now, so it's a good thing we had time… such a privilege to explore that with you.

Finding a Good Stopping Place

This dreamwork example was done in a group with some of my students of focusing-oriented dreamwork, and the conversation continued. After the session, which took well over an hour, we discussed how to find a good stopping place. I have included the salient parts of the conversation here because this is an issue that comes up often when working with dreams, especially if time is limited.

STUDENT: What would you do if you only had a certain amount of time, and you didn't get to a good place in that time?

T: I always try to leave enough time for dreamwork. Typical therapy sessions are an hour or less, but for dreamwork I like to have 90 minutes, because it's not really a process you can rush. I had actually a fairly good sense of where the dreamwork needed to go, but any sort of rushing through any of those steps probably would not have worked. It has its own timing. If there is less time with a dream like that, it would feel unfinished I think. There was a place where the client entered into the world of that dream and it felt different, not as creepy. That would have been an okay landing place. If I didn't have time to get to the place where it felt finished, I would try to find a good landing place. I want people feel the process as constructive, and not something they would worry about doing another time. There may be times when it doesn't end well, but I try to avoid that by making sure there is enough time.

Because this is a teaching setting, I have the opportunity to ask the client: "What would you say if you had stopped where you looked around and found it had changed, would that have been an okay place to end?"

C: I thought that was going to be an ending point because I didn't feel like there was anywhere else to go. It had already changed my understanding of the dream, and my feeling of what was back there. There's a huge difference between how I felt then versus how I felt at the end of the session, but it already was like a shift. Something had changed, so that was good. But then at the end of the session it was an overwhelming bodily change. It was interesting because we both knew it was important to make connection and I tried to let the dream move forward, I kept trying to cross over but I could tell it wasn't working. And finally at the end I thought well, don't cross over, just merge.

T: I love that the dream doesn't let you make it up. It's like an authentic process and it doesn't let you pretend. And it seems like the solution comes from being receptive but also letting it happen. The smooshing into the glass and having it become liquid – you can tell that's authentic, you're not going to make that up. And that ending where you get flooded with relief and there are tears, and

you are filled with something that's positive, that's the place we are trying to get to. I'm glad we got there.
c: Me too. (laughter)
s: Ask the client: You have had dreams a bit similar to this, does this process make you feel differently about all those other dreams?
c: Mirrors and younger versions of me are common themes. It doesn't change those individual dreams, but it feels like it changes my relationship to the dreaming world as a whole. Like I'm holding it much differently.
s: The dream would not let her be inauthentic. I'm wondering if you have times when people are fudging it?
t: Often. People try to be good clients, but the thing is, it's very obvious. Because we are tracking the felt sense, it's impossible to make those shifts without being authentic. People can make up a fantasy, but you can feel that it's disconnected. It can be playful and fun, but it doesn't make the felt shift happen. People might try that for awhile but they are shortchanging themselves. Most people quickly realize that it's better to simply say so when it's not working because it's not going to go anywhere if they confabulate.
s: Do you tell them directly when they do it?
t: Not directly, because I don't want them to feel like they are doing it wrong. But when I sense it, I will acknowledge them and then guide them back to the dream or their body, back somewhere that felt authentic to me. I won't make them wrong, I just won't follow it up. I can tell it's not leading anywhere.

A few days later, the client wrote:

That was such a wonderful session for me. I still feel clearly the woman in the white dress. She feels held in a way now; even if she is in a dark place she is not alone. There is a sense that she can finally breathe. Even though she is still sad, she is also overwhelmed with gratitude because she had no hope for so long that anyone or I should ever hold her in this way, it didn't occur to her as even possible. She is stunned to realize she is worthy of being held and being loved. I guess that is the clearest thing: I can feel that she has suffered, she is suffering, but now she is held and loved. In a way she can feel her pain more freely and safely and know she is loved, like crying in someone's arms. It's a really beautiful feeling.

Even typing that I had some memories resurface, I can remember being cut off from someone's love and deciding that I would have to keep my aching closed away in a box in my heart and pretend it didn't exist. That even gives the white dress new meaning. It was the first person I fell in love with, and when he didn't love me, I tried to pretend I didn't care, I ignored my sadness and loneliness. And now that I mention that, I realize I've had several dreams of this guy over the past month.

I wonder what other parts of myself I could find behind the mirror.

We discussed the dream a bit more in a later conversation. It felt like a place she could revisit. I wanted to know which side of the dream divide she was on – and she said she would much rather stay with the dream itself while working on it because wondering about its connections to her life would take her out of the process, and possibly confuse things for her. As it was, one of the main waking life connections, the discovery of a part of herself that still held sadness and loneliness from a lost love, came to her spontaneously a few days after working with the dream. And that part of her felt held and loved after waiting for a very long time.

References

Badenoch, B. (2018). *The heart of trauma: Healing the embodied brain in the context of relationships.* New York, NY: W. W. Norton & Company.

Benedetti F., Poletti S., Radaelli D., Ranieri R., Genduso V., Cavallotti S., et al. (2015). Right hemisphere neural activations in the recall of waking fantasies and of dreams. *Journal of Sleep Research*, 24(5), 576e82.

Gendlin, E. T. (2012). Implicit precision. In Z. Radman (Ed.). *Knowing without thinking: The theory of the background in philosophy of mind.* Basingstoke: Palgrave Macmillan.

Laughlin, C. D. (2013). Dreaming and reality: A neuroanthropological account. *International Journal of Transpersonal Studies*, 32(1), 64–78.

Laughlin, C. D., & Rock, A. J. (2014). What can we learn from shamans' dreaming? A cross-cultural exploration. *Dreaming*, 24(4), 233–252.

McGilchrist, I. (2009). *The master and his emissary: The divided brain and the making of the Western world.* New Haven and London: Yale University Press.

Siegel, A. (2016). Developmental life cycle method. In Lewis, J. & Krippner, S. (Eds.), *Working with Dreams and PTSD Nightmares: 14 Approaches for Psychotherapists and Counselors.* Santa Barbara, CA & Denver, CO: Praeger.

8 The Central Quest

Finding the Life Force Inherent in All Dreams

> *Dreams pass into the reality of action. From the actions stems the dream again; and this interdependence produces the highest form of living.*
>
> Anaïs Nin

"A dream is alive," according to Gendlin (2012a). If one were to single out the overarching purpose for working with our dreams, he would say it is to locate and embody the sense of aliveness inherent in every dream. Gendlin (1992) believed that every dream brings some form of 'help' that contains within it the energy to propel the dreamer's life forward, possibly, as Nin (1969) suggests, toward "the highest form of living." After more than 20 years of working with dreams, I have come to believe in Gendlin's emphasis on embodying the dream's life force. I did not start out with this view, but was suspicious of overly optimistic or too-easy answers. One of my first dreamwork teachers said to approach a dream by starting with the most striking or intense image in the dream, and while this is impactful, it is not as gentle or affirming as Gendlin's approach. Finding and aligning with the helpful forces in a dream allows the dreamer to feel more secure, more resourced, more able to move forward into the challenging terrain that may lie ahead. If you are undertaking a difficult journey, it makes sense to equip yourself with as many resources as possible

Forms of Help and How to Find It

In some dreams, the helpful dream elements are obvious ones such as children, beautiful objects, characters with strength and loving presence, white or colorful light or magnificent animals. For example, one of my clients dreamed of a large black woman whose character felt like the archetypal good mother; my client curled up in her ample lap to be soothed and rocked and told everything was going to be okay. This is a very obvious version of help in a dream, and an example of a dream that does its work on its own, requiring no interpretation from a therapist. I have found that dreams like this often come when they are needed most, and are a gift from the psyche. Other dreams may seem universally dark or scary and in such dreams, help can be much harder to find. Gendlin (1992) suggested that even in such dreams, there will be help:

> some change in the usual set, something extra with positive energy – something so that we don't just tackle a stuck issue in the way the person always does ... Of course we could expect such help from any novel, odd and very noticeable things that the dream brings. For example, if there are two sculptured bowls, or some odd box with sticks coming out of it – or anything of that sort – of course we would attend to anything like that before we tackled the main issue.

In fact, using the help involves not just attending to the positive energy in such a dream element, but also feeling it in our bodies, trying to enter directly into the perspective of the helpful character or object and then carrying that with us as we journey further into the dream. We can use the help as an ally, a source of strength or a guide to help us find our way forward in the very life challenges to which the dream is referring.

One client I worked with found help in a very strange place. *In the dream, there are miners pushing explosive tubes into the earth, and although the dreamer insists this is very dangerous, the miners persist, pushing down hard, even as something deep in the ground pushes back.* The feeling of "push-back" took some time to find and it took a few iterations to find just the right way to feel and express this dream element. Eventually it became a very reliable feeling in the client's chest that remains an ally in every decision he makes. He used to agonize over every decision, tended to be a martyr, and even after making a choice, would second-guess himself over and over. The "push-back" feeling took away all the uncertainty and self-doubt and replaced it with clarity, confidence and assertiveness that has literally changed the way this client approaches his life.

Gabby and the "Holy Trinity"

The following is an extended clinical example provided by Sue Cornfield, a clinical psychologist in Cape Town. She attended a workshop where I spoke with clinicians in South Africa about working with the dreams and nightmares of their clients. The ideas presented on finding and embodying helpful dream elements, as well as entering the dream and allowing it to continue, were new to many of the participants. One reason for presenting this example is to show how dreamwork can assist over a longer course of therapy, with the dream changes indicating clinical progress. It also illustrates that transformative dream work is not a unique skill, nor one that is difficult to learn and practice. This is not to take away anything from Cornfield and the dedication and clinical sensitivity she brings to the case of Gabby, who was willing and honored to have her real identity and story told here. As you will see in this example, the "help" in a dream can be a healing image all by itself, and one that can have tremendous staying power. In Gabby's dream, the help was a "holy trinity" of cat, child and mother that became a living, healing image in her quest to recover from a deep mother wound that colored all of her relationships, including her relationship with herself.

Gabby started therapy at age 40 for help ending a 10-year affair with a married man. At the time, she was an art teacher, and lived alone. She attended therapy for four years, two to three times per week at first, and tapering to weekly as her therapy progressed. Over the course of the therapy, she left the art school to run her own courses, formed a solid, loving relationship, moved out of town to live on a farm, and most importantly, came to terms with her lifelong challenges in her relationship with her mother.

According to Cornfield, Gabby's main difficulties revolved around an almost non-existent relationship with her mother, a wounded and narcissistic woman. In her childhood, Gabby could not recall any holding, comforting, mirroring or guidance from her mother who struggled with depression, frequently threatened suicide and made at least one attempt. Gabby's mother also had an eating disorder and gave her daughter the message that thinness was essential for acceptance. Gabby's mother used all her spare time, when not working as a teacher, to study; she earned four undergraduate and three post-graduate degrees. Gabby's image of her mother is of her back, sitting at the dining room table, head in her books. Gabby was the unseen child, the good girl who never made waves – the mirroring, comforting, mothering child.

Gabby was a tall skinny girl with curly brown hair, who remembers her childhood self as desperately lonely, confused and sad. She often closeted herself in her room. Her mother was only ever on the edge of her world, too caught up in her own dramas to tune into her child. Her father, whom Gabby described as an alcoholic, weak, but practical man, looked after the physical needs of Gabby and her brother, but did not provide much emotional support. As an adult, Gabby's relationship with her mother consisted of Gabby spending hour after hour listening to her mother talk about herself. As she listened, Gabby had a "falling in" feeling inside that became so unbearable she ultimately decided to stop spending time with her mother altogether.

In therapy, Gabby came across as an un-mothered child who needed to find her voice and be heard. The married man she was involved with set himself up as a guru and she idolized him. She left him and grieved the parting painfully. Her process has involved a great deal of grieving, including anger, deep sorrow and longing for the mother she never had and for her legitimate child needs that were never met. She grieved having to be such a good and mothering child, the ongoing fear of her mother committing suicide, the tyranny of having to be thin, her years of amenorrhea and concerns around fertility, and more. She was desperately in need of empathic holding, a secure attachment and emotional regulation. Cornfield said that over the course of the nearly four years, Gabby shifted quite substantially. What helped was her strong life force in the direction of healing herself, openness and ability to reflect, and a natural gift for the process of sensing inside. She explored many avenues in her healing process, including art, poetry, dance and ritual. However, the dream work with Cornfield was instrumental in catalyzing the process. The following dream, which Gabby had after having no contact with her mother for more than two years, helped her learn how to effectively mother her own child-self and find the right way for her to be in relationship with her mother.

Gabby's dream: *I was travelling to New York and arrived at the hotel. They were in a flap at the hotel, short of staff and needing extra waitresses that evening. I agreed to waitress for them. Then I went for a walk, came across a cat and stopped to talk to it. A little girl came out of the house and I chatted to her as well. It was her cat. Then the mom came out of the house and because she saw that the child and the cat trusted me, she offered to take me sightseeing. I decided to do that rather than waitress (and wondered why I had agreed to it in the first place). Then my mother's family came into the room and sat in a huge circle. Everybody had a chance to tell a story or sing a song. There was a couple who were singing a song and when they got to a certain part of the song, one of the women in the circle fell onto the floor and started crying. The person next to me said: "Don't worry, she always reacts like that to those words. Don't pay her any attention." The woman's tone had no care or concern, was just matter-of-fact. One of the women stood up and started talking about her printmaking class she was going to give the next day. She said, "It is an expensive activity this," and I shared with her some different techniques I had used to do printing… The phone rang and woke me up.*

Cornfield said,

> I was struck by the difference in the warmth and engagement of her interaction with the cat, child and mother and the lack of warmth, empathy and engagement in the circle with the collapsed woman, which I consider all to be parts of herself. With the new understanding from Leslie Ellis's workshop, I thought the cat/child/mother might represent help in the dream and I wondered if entering the dream might bring some clarity and forward movement.

First, Cornfield explored associations with Gabby, in particular her felt sense of the characters. The mother in the dream was kind and open, as was the little girl. Gabby said this was a warm, sturdy, steady mother who looked out for her child. She found the couple who sang together to be strange: "Why would they sing that song if they knew that every time it would make her cry?" Gabby identified with the pain of the woman who collapsed on the floor weeping and was curious about the fact that the others ignored the woman in her distress: Why did the people not do something? Why did they always let it happen? Why didn't I say something like, 'Please don't always sing that song, it makes me sad?'

Cornfield wrote,

> I saw a lot of interesting aspects to this dream which I could have explored further but, given the warmth of the maternal figure it seemed natural to bring this forward as it clearly represented some of the 'help' in the dream. I wondered out aloud: Could the cat, child, mother have or know what the weeping lady needed? Gabby's eyes widened with surprise and she exclaimed, 'Yes! Even if just the cat went to her!' There was an energy and aliveness in her expression, then a thoughtful silence as she connected with the sad woman, and said, 'She needs comfort, gentleness and warmth.'

Entering the Dream

One of the techniques I taught Cornfield and the others in the workshop is to ask dreamers to re-enter their dream and allow it to continue. Cornfield tried this with Gabby, allowing her to choose her own right way forward in the dream. *She entered the dream in the circle. The cat went to the woman and snuggled into her. The cat grounded her and she sat up. The little girl brought her a flower from outside and sat with her back against the woman's back, reading a book. The little girl's innocence helped the woman. The woman felt seen and heard. The mother made eye contact and the woman smiled. The mother then helped the woman onto her chair. Then archangel Michael came in and stood in front of the couple and told them to stop singing. There was a blueish light in the room. Gabby felt she needed to tell a story, which she said quietly in her imagination. She reported that the woman was calm now. Then Gabby gave a shift-breath, opened her eyes and came out of the dream. She felt calm and said she had an urge to immerse herself in water.*

The Following Sessions

After this process, Gabby reported feeling calm, peaceful, solid and grounded. She had been thinking about her mother and she was considering connecting with her. She felt there were still issues to work through but what struck Cornfield was that *the anxiety around it all seemed to have lifted.* At this point in the session, Gabby pulled a photograph out of her handbag of herself as a child, taken when she was a similar age to the child in the dream. Gabby said she felt such tenderness towards her child-self. "It feels like the first time I'm relating to her as an adult, the first time I'm connecting to her as adult me. Before I felt *like* the child; now I'm the adult and I *see* the child."

The dream continued to speak to Gabby often throughout the week. The cat, child, mother and Cornfield, as well as the process of working with the dream, and its sense of safety – all of this stayed with her. The cat 'brings me closer to myself.' She said the two who were singing had disintegrated into ash, and this felt as though it dissipated the negative charge she had held in relation to her parents. She spoke of intense grief around lost innocence, a deep regret that she always had to hold it all together and could never just be a little girl who could play and have fun. She said,

> There was something about the cat trusting me, then the child and then the mother – it means they saw good in me – there was something in me that was trustworthy. I was so good as a teenager, but it was like my parents didn't see me or trust me.

Gabby continued to feel a new sense of identification with her adult self rather than the child, and she had an impulse to take care of her child-self in tangible, specific ways:

> I want to buy her clothes, play with her, make her feel safe, put her on my lap, cuddle her before she goes to sleep, tell her she is capable and brave and clever and funny, let her run around naked if she wants to and teach her that her body is beautiful. I'll tell her she is a good girl and it doesn't matter if she makes mistakes and I won't mind if she is naughty every now and again. I would tell her it doesn't matter if she can't hit a ball and I'd listen to her nightmares.

She ended by saying she wanted to make "something magnificent" for her and the cat. When Cornfield commented that Gabby somehow was looking more feminine, she said, "The feminine holy trinity of the cat, child, mother… I like it."

Gabby had another dream: *She was walking past a shop and her mother was in it, and she had a choice to keep walking but decided to enter the shop and casually say hello. She noticed her mother was smoking again.* What was striking was how neutral her feelings were around her mother in the dream when throughout her life these emotions had been intense and difficult. Had she seen her mother in a shop, she would have run in the opposite direction, her stomach in knots. Gabby said, "It feels like a whole lot of clearing has happened and something has been released. It is up to me to decide whether to see her or not. *I can't find that desperation in my body anymore.*" Upon waking, Gabby felt relief that when she saw her mother in the dream she "didn't freak out." There was no deep love or connection; it was calm and neutral. It felt equally fine to choose to go in or walk past. She did not have her customary reaction even to the smoking, realizing she that she could have compassion but ultimately was not responsible for her mother's health.

"It's not my fault and I can't do anything about it. I don't have to be the good daughter and fix it. I don't have to go back into a relationship because it will make her feel better; it will be because I choose to… *I feel so different.* There is that wonderful sense of freedom that I can choose."

In the session, Gabby said she had been able to tend to a lot of papercuts that had been left open, and that she felt a sense of completeness. The artwork she brought depicted her child self at about age 6, the same age as the little girl in the dream. Gabby said she felt love for the child for the first time. That night after the session, she dreamt: *I took off all my clothes and was swimming in the most beautiful ocean. The water was flat and felt perfect on my skin.* This dream completed the desire Gabby had experienced in her initial dream work to get into the water. In the next session, Gabby started by saying that it felt like something had clicked into place. Something had strengthened inside her and she said it started with the dream.

Cornfield felt that for Gabby, entering the dream and engaging with the most important dream elements seemed to have facilitated a process where Gabby was able to begin to mother herself, to feel stronger and happier inside, to feel more adult and to make choices on her own behalf with freedom and without guilt. A mark of her transformation was her ability to be with her mother in a whole new way, to visit with her partner and listen to her mother talk about herself for the entire visit, and to find it hilarious. Gabby said her mother asked nothing about them at all. However, she did not collapse inside. It was light-hearted and fine, and she said, "Nothing inside yearns for anything else." She and her partner laughed for an hour afterwards. "The situation hasn't changed but I have changed."

Help Can Come from Unlikely Places

In the above examples, the help was relatively easy to find. Gabby's "holy trinity" felt warm and accepting and was clearly a source of positive affirmation. Even the "push-back" help from the example earlier in the chapter was obvious to the client, though it may not have been so clear to an outside observer that this particular element contained the helpful new energy in the dream. Finding the dream's life force is a bit more challenging when working with those dreams where help seems entirely absent. Gendlin (2012b) would say that regardless of how dark a dream may appear, the help is in there somewhere, but we may need to work a little harder to find it. An example he liked to use is a woman's dream of a wounded turtle that is limping along the road, entrails dragging. Because there was no help to be found in this image, Gendlin asked, "What would a healthy turtle be like?" and this brought a shift. With any damaged or wounded dream element, it can be helpful to ask what its usual strength or virtue would be, and to ask the dreamer to sense into what this might mean for them. This way of working may seem as though it is forcing something positive to happen, and I would suggest that if it feels that way to the client, then it's not the right move. But it is something to try in your search for help.

I would add that in some dreams, there truly may be no help to be found, such as in the recurrent nightmares of those who have experienced severe trauma. I will discuss such dreams in more detail in the chapter on nightmares, but for now will briefly offer the solution I have found to locating help when working with such dreams. I think even these disturbing and seemingly unhelpful dreams serve a purpose, and are part of the body's attempt to come to terms with the trauma. However, the dreamer can become so terrified by the dream images that they wake up before the dream can complete, and are afraid to go back to sleep and dream the same thing again. It can become a vicious cycle. In such cases, I believe the help is not located in the dream itself, but in its completion, in what it *implies*. Allowing such a dream to continue is delicate work, but I have found that it can have a dramatic effect, changing and sometimes completely stopping recurrent nightmares that have been plaguing the dreamer for years.

Gendlin is not the only one who thinks dreams are universally helpful. Taylor (1992), a well-known dream worker who spent six decades working with dreams said, "The single most important conclusion I have come to in my work is that all dreams come in the service of health and wholeness." Gabby's dream provides an example of how a dream can bring just what is needed to help resolve the most difficult emotional challenges in a person's life. And even when the "help" is less dramatic, it can serve bolster the dreamer and provide what's needed, such as inner strength or courage, that will enable the dreamer to integrate the more challenging aspects of their dreams. This is why, early on in the process of working with a dream, it is a good idea to locate and embody the help, to have it there as fuel or strength for the journey ahead both in working the dream, and in life.

References

Gendlin, E. T. (1992). Three learnings since the dreambook. *The Folio,* 11(1), 25–30.
Gendlin, E. T. (2012a). "Philosophy, focusing and dreams," recorded phone seminar available at www.focusingresources.com.
Gendlin, E. T. (2012b). Body dreamwork. In P. McNamara and D. Barrett, (Eds.). *Encyclopedia of sleep and dreams.* Westport, CT: Praeger.
Nin, A. 1969. *The diary of Anaïs Nin,* vol. 3, p. 91. London: Harvest Books.
Taylor, J. (1992). *The wisdom of your dreams.* New York, NY: Jeremy P. Acher/Penguin.

9 Avenues of Exploration
Visual Art and Technology

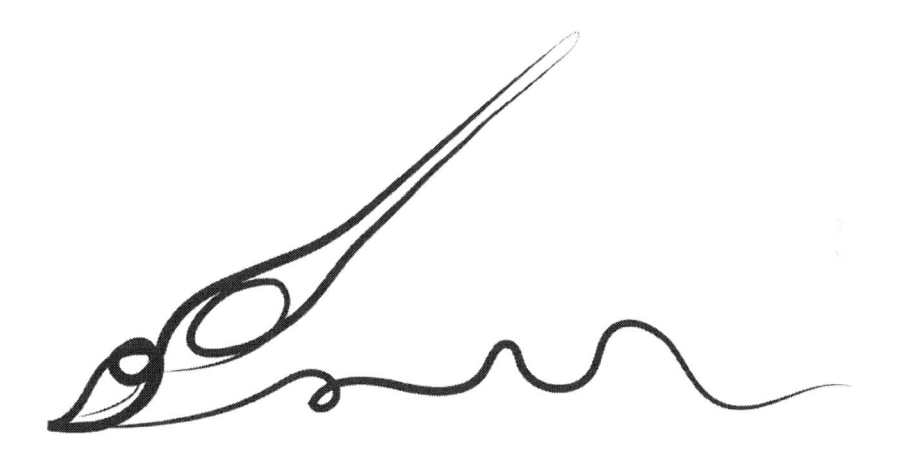

I dream my painting and I paint my dream.

Vincent Willem van Gogh

Sometimes even after working with a dream, aspects of it remain a mystery. A visual representation can drop those missing pieces into place, and it also provides a lasting record of the dream that both the dreamer and therapist can absorb at a glance. Using art – often drawing, but also sculpture, video or other media – can facilitate the dreamer's further exploration of their dream, within or outside of therapy. It is also a helpful way to engage with a dream over time, which is especially useful if it feels like a big, important dream. In this chapter, I offer examples of working with a dream visually, and explore how dream depiction may be expanded in the future as visual technology advances.

Working with Art and Images

Dreams most often come to us in the form of images, sometimes incredibly rich in detail and complexity. When we wake up, we usually try to capture our dreams by making a story out of them. However, this human tendency to form a narrative to make sense of our experience does not always do justice to the dream, and sometimes truly alters it. Visual art speaks a language that is closer to dreaming, so it is often helpful to ask our clients to depict their dreams by sketching or painting them, and in the process, new information and insight often emerges.

The idea of painting or drawing our dream images is not a new one; dreams have likely been inspiring artistic creation since mankind was first able to make images. Jung was the first, however, to use the visual representation of dreams as part of a psychotherapeutic process. Much of his dream art is now published in his *Red Book* and the Jungian community has been able to make a deep dive into the complexity of his dream experience. However, for most therapists, the use of art in dreamwork can be as simple as asking the client to draw a quick sketch of their dream in the session.

Walter Berry is a specialist in the visual approach to dreamwork. He said he first started using art in his dreamwork practice a decade ago when a woman brought an incredibly complex dream that changed with each telling. It was so confusing, he had asked her to tell it three times. Then he asked if she could do a sketch of the dream, just to help him organize the dream image for himself. With the picture, he could make sense of the dream and begin to work with it, and since then, asking the dreamer to draw their dream has become a central part of how he works.

The biggest obstacle to working with dreams visually, according to Berry, is the reluctance people have to drawing their dreams. Many people are concerned about their lack of artistic ability, and it can take a bit of cajoling to help them get started. Stick figures and rough outlines are just as effective for dreamwork as any other kind of image, so Berry deliberately provides examples of his own rudimentary dream art to increase the comfort level of any would-be dream artist. He also usually asks people to sketch dreams in session rather than doing artwork at home and bringing it in because people tend to fuss more over the quality of the images they create if they have time.

Berry showed me an example of a sketch of *a woman's dream journey in a submarine which takes her to a beach. She gets out and walks across the sand to two underground compounds where she lives. They are circular, side by side and surrounded by barbed wire.* When she looks at the drawing, the image of a map of her journey was immediately associated with her mother's breasts, and from there, themes related to security and lack of nurturing arose for her; the discussion deepened. The point of this example is that surprising things emerge from the images, important themes that might not have come up in the verbal telling of the dream.

In another example Berry provides, *a woman dreams that she is blind and has to get through a maze. A secret service agent's face appears in the dream, and he is part of a network of people that are helping her navigate the maze.* In her drawing, the network is represented simply, by a series of connected dots. Berry always asks first about the emotions in the dream because it takes the dreamer away from the tendency to create a narrative and underscores the fact that dreams are predominantly emotional experiences. The dreamer responds to his query with some analysis about the man in the dream as an animus figure, helping her navigate life. In the meantime, Berry is counting the dots. There are 17, and just in case this is meaningful, he asks, "What happened when you were 17?" The woman bursts into tears and said that was how old she was when she seriously contemplated suicide. This led to a conversation about how the internal male figure has been with her all along, and in a way, saved her from killing herself. Berry's other favorite question to ask of a dreamer is, "Why did you have this dream, and why now?" This opened up an additional layer of conversation, all of it made so much deeper and more relevant with the backdrop of her adolescent suicidal episode.

I wonder, was the dream actually referring to this intense time in her life, or did the number 17 crop up simply because of the drawing? Was it coincidence, or the unconscious at work unearthing key details? Berry suggests that both can be true – the dream is bringing the key association, or the drawing is, or both. There is often evidence that the dream is the catalyst because once you find one key, Berry says there are many more instances of the same theme that become apparent. It's not critical to pick up on every clue or even every dream. The important themes repeat themselves within dreams, and in subsequent dreams until the dreamer gets what they are trying to convey.

Dreamwork as Performance Art

Mark Blagrove and Julia Lockheart have taken the use of visual art and dreamwork a step further and created a new kind of performance art they call *DreamsID*. Dreams have long been a source of material for artistic creation. The reason for including the performance dream art project here is because of the way it informs dream therapy – it shows how valuable it can be to have a visual record of a dream, one you can revisit, share and replay like a movie.

I can provide a personal example of the dream art experience because Blagrove and Lockheart were kind enough to walk me through this process using a dream I named The Tapestry of Life: *I am on the top floor of an old stone building that is open in the middle with a staircase spiraling down the entire perimeter. I am about to turn the corner and head down the stairs when the tapestry on the wall beside me moves a little and catches my attention. It was once red but is so old it has faded to an orange color. It is so richly detailed I can't make out the images on it. I become lucid enough in the dream to realize I'm dreaming, and the whole experience feels profound. Because of this, I try to take a closer look at the tapestry to make out what's on it. There is a tree, and maybe a river, and so much more, but a feeling that it will take time and a particular kind of attention from me to see what's there.*

The day after having this dream, I was teaching a workshop on focusing and dreamwork to a group of researchers in the UK, and so had a chance to work with it when we paired up to practice. (If there is an odd number of participants, I usually step in and become one of the participants.) Guided by an adept participant, I re-entered the dreamscape, and more came to me about the dream that

90 *Avenues of Exploration*

Figure 9.1 "Tapestry of Life" dream. Illustration by Julia Lockheart

I had forgotten. There was now a group of people waiting to see the tapestry, so I had to move on, rather reluctantly. I also felt how the tapestry was like the felt sense in focusing in the way that it did not appear all that striking at first, but would open up and reveal more as I patiently attended to it. I also discovered, in revisiting the dream, that if you looked at the tapestry from a different angle, an entirely different scene would appear; each angle showed something different. It gave me a tangible image of how in dreamwork, and in life in general, so much depends on perspective.

A few weeks later, at a dream conference, I attended a session where we were invited to make watercolor sketches of one of our dreams. I attempted to paint my tapestry dream and found it very difficult to depict the tapestry itself since I didn't really know what was on it. I could not leave such a central feature of the dream blank, so I randomly added some images, the tree, a fountain, some animals... and as I was drawing, I had the sense that the tapestry was coming to life, that the images were lifting off the fabric, and the tree was growing off the edges. It was as if the dream itself had come alive.

This brings me back to the work of Blagrove and Lockheart, who worked with this dream as well. Lockheart is a skilled artist who is interested in the interaction between art and language. As I spoke with Blagrove about the dream, Lockheart painted it. In her process she uses the paragraph structure of pages from Freud's *The Interpretation of Dreams* for the production of her artworks. After finding suitable shapes in the text that fit the narrative, she draws and paints onto the page. She said that as she works, "Words from the page seem to jump up from the text into the image, providing associations from Freud's writings into my capturing of the dream."

The pair pioneered this method at the British Science Festival in 2016 and have since been invited to many other prestigious venues to showcase their work, including the Freud Museum. It has captured the attention of the dreaming community as a way to engage the public in their dreams. They provide participants with a high-quality Giclée print of the artwork, and this enables the dreamers to continue to revisit and engage with their dreams. Blagrove said the process invites ongoing engagement with the dream image, and discussion with others via the artwork. Lockheart spoke of how deeply personal and intimate the dream conversations in this process often become, surprising the dreamer with the intensity of emotion that arises. She recalls one particularly poignant session in which the dreamer, whose only memory of her mother was of her funeral, brought a dream encounter of her mother. She has come to treasure the resulting image of her dream, and the sense of lost connection it restored for her. The DreamsID process has led to a theory that dream-telling increases empathy between the listener and dreamer (Blagrove, Carr, Jones & Lockheart, 2018).

There are many things a dream therapist can extract from these examples. My tapestry dream experience is a perfect illustration of how a dream stays alive and can change and evolve as one works with it. It also demonstrates how depicting the dream visually can enrich the process as well as provide a record of it that can bring the sense of the dream back in an instant, in a way that is much more efficient and evocative than rereading the original written account. One of my strongest impressions after looking at the image Lockheart created is that in her rendition, the tapestry is bursting with life. The tree has come to dominate the image, which is not an accurate depiction of my actual dream, but conveys the feeling of it very well. The image Lockheart created as Blagrove and I discussed the dream is a combination of my original dream, her impressions in hearing me tell it, and the dreamwork I do as I answer Blagrove's questions, mainly aimed at fleshing out the visual details of the dream.

92 *Avenues of Exploration*

Figure 9.2 "Big Ben" lucid dream. Illustration by Julia Lockheart

The more time I spend with the dream tapestry, the more life seems to flow from it. I can also see something new that Lockheart's drawing makes apparent: the roots of the tree and the water go down into the depths of the interior; the depths are the source of all the life, though what is down there is not visible. It feels important that she added a flow of water to extend beyond the tapestry as I can see it flowing down and watering the tree roots. I have a sense that this dream will continue to evolve for me, and that having the drawings, both my own and Lockheart's, will keep it alive and present in a way that enhances the written account. I see the original text, and also how much has changed now that I have gotten to know the image better.

Visualizing Dreams: What the Future Holds

At a science and dreaming symposium at UCLA in October, 2018, Blagrove and Lockheart demonstrated DreamsID via the internet, with Blagrove leading a symposium participant through her dream while Lockheart, at home in the UK, drew the image for the audience at UCLA. The participant, Emi, was a student who had just finished an intense exam period and was preparing to head home for the holidays. She dreamt that she and some of her friends from her home town were visiting London, and were near the Big Ben clock tower when she felt herself being lifted. She looked around and saw that everyone around her was also rising off the ground. She became lucid in this dream, and had a lot of fun with it: *We were flying and spinning around Big Ben, like in the movie Peter Pan, the famous scene where they are flying around. It was like a picturesque version of that, swirling and doing loops. I could look down at the whole world and city, the contrast of bright lights with the dark night sky. My vision was blurred black and yellow with lots of noise. It was freezing cold. The wind was going really fast. I could feel the cold, but it was like an adrenaline rush. We kept going further out into the ocean. I could control everything.*

A frequent lucid dreamer, she knew how to end such dreams: she dove straight into the ocean and woke up. She is also a video game player and her dream demonstrates the affinity between gaming and lucidity in dreams. Researcher Jayne Gackenbach (2006) has explored the link between lucid dreaming and video game play, and notes that the focused attention required in gaming (and meditation) is associated with lucid dreaming. More recently (2011), she conducted a study supporting her theory that the immersion by today's youth in a wide range of media, not just video games, is associated with dream lucidity and control. This control can provide some protection against nightmares, particularly for male 'high-end' gamers. The frequent practice in a simulated environment where they successfully fight off attackers can be translated into their dream experience, empowering them to take the same kind of control in their dreams.

The relationship between dreams and gaming is just one way in which technology and dreamwork are beginning to intersect. At the UCLA symposium, an eclectic group of professionals representing computer engineering, neuroscience, anthropology, dream science, and film and television production wrestled with possible ways to improve the depiction of dreams in the future. Currently, we tend to use text and occasionally art to depict dreams for therapy or research. However, this is a poor representation because dreams are much closer to movies. If we all had the resources of an animation studio like Pixar, we could show others exactly what our dreams look like, but of course this is impractical. Jeff Burke of the UCLA school of theater, film and television demonstrated some animated graphic production tools that might make efficient reproduction of dreamscapes more feasible in the future. He showed the group animation in 2.5 rather than 3 dimensions to economically capture some of the motion and spatial relationships so often featured in dreams. Already, we can choose from a vast array of characters and settings available in digital format, and these could be combined to depict our dreamscapes. Possibly dreamworkers of the future will be able to use software to construct a basic movie of a client's dream.

At a dream engineering symposium at the MIT media lab in early 2019, researchers demonstrated early stage technology that could actually capture and display rudimentary images and semantic information directly from a person's mind. Someday we may be able to capture and replay our dreams, or intervene *within* them. Already a group of researchers at MIT is doing just that: monitoring sleep stages and introducing physical stimulation, scent or other input in an attempt to influence dream experience. MIT researcher Adam Horowitz dubbed this "incepting" dreams, a take-off from the movie *Inception* in which the main character is able to enter people's dreams to steal secrets or plant ideas. Emerging technology may change how dreamwork is done, and spark its resurgence by making it more relevant for today's youth.

Paul Lippman (2000/2013) is one of many authors on dreams who laments the steady decline in modern Western culture's interest in dreams. He suggests this may be in part because our ancestors had very few entertainment options, so their dream life would likely stand out as particularly imaginative compared with their daily life. By contrast, today we are bombarded with stimulation, and exposed to virtual realities of stunning quality, which has rendered our dreams more ordinary and less compelling by comparison. Still, dreams have one major advantage over movies, video games and such: they are intensely personal. They depict vivid, sometimes surreal landscapes that carry emotional charge and memory traces that are our very own, and they appear on the screen of our mind's eye, played for us alone. Sometimes they are so moving and creative, we are compelled to tell someone, and the social impulse they foster is emerging as one of the newest theories about dream function. Moving images from our mind's eye to this world, however this is done, enhances and extends the dreamwork process in helpful and sometimes surprising ways.

References

Mark Blagrove, Michelle Carr, Alex Jones, and Julia Lockheart, (June, 2018). *A new theory of dream function: Telling dreams enhances empathy towards the dreamer.* Poster presentation at the International Association for the Study of Dreams conference, Scottsdale, AZ.

Gackenbach, J. I. (2006). Video game play and lucid dreams: Implications for the development of consciousness. *Dreaming,* 16(2), 96–110.

Gackenbach, J. I. (2011). Electronic media and lucid-control dreams: Morning after reports. *Dreaming,* 19(1), 1–6.

Lippman, P. (2000/2013). *Nocturnes: On listening to dreams.* New York, NY: Routledge.

10 The Inner Journey
Dreams and the Body

At night the dream has me, but in the morning I say I had a dream.

James Hillman

I got up before dawn to begin the full days' journey from my home in Deep Cove near Vancouver to Malinalco, a village about a two-hour drive through the rugged terrain southwest of Mexico City. In the fading dusk, I finally reached the village, quietly alive, its market stalls filled with flowers, candles, sweet bread and sugar skulls in preparation for the upcoming Day of the Dead. The following morning, here, in the sanctuary of a garden retreat on the outskirts of town, sitting with a small group of dreamers in an open room with floor to ceiling windows facing towering red clay bluffs, I am working a dream, holding its multiple images in my body. I am so immersed in the experience, I don't notice I'm sweating, don't hear the snapping buzz of the cicadas or braying donkeys that punctuate our work. Instead my attention is fully occupied with trying to hold a *composite* of several *anchor points* from my dream, fully engaged in the practice of *embodied imagination* (EI), as developed by Robert Bosnak and his colleague Jill Fischer.

Throughout the week we spend doing dreamwork sessions led by Bosnak, group members explore a stunning variety of dream landscapes. We are a small eclectic group composed of therapists, artists, students and an inventor, but we feel more alike than different in our willingness to inhabit the world of our dreams. I am an experienced body dreamworker from the tradition of focusing, which shares some common features of EI, in particular its careful attention to the bodily felt sense a dream brings. However, focusing is a gentle, more purely phenomenological approach, not so structured or intense as EI, nor quite as demanding for the dreamer or dreamworker. However, it is the gentleness of the focusing process that gives it the disarming power to open up places in the dream that may otherwise remain defended.

Experiencing the Dream from the Inside

There are pros and cons to any practice that applies great pressure; while the effort required is considerable, so is the potential for transformation. Bosnak developed the practice of EI with careful attention to how a dreamer can embody specific elements of their dream in a way these dream presences become powerful agents of change. In EI, dreamers are guided to sink into the atmosphere surrounding each chosen dream element, noticing smells, sounds, surroundings, and also what is particularly salient about the dream elements or characters themselves. For example, in my dreamwork session, the first element I worked with was a pair of young men running through the streets of downtown Vancouver at night. In my dreamscape, this area of town was practically deserted and it was dark but not impossible to see. The men are opposites in a way, one dark and fiercely competitive, the other light and playful. Both are young strong runners flying down the road at great speed, and as I am describing the scene, I can suddenly feel their legs as if they are my own. I have made a spontaneous *transit* into the body of the dream figures and am guided to remain in that perspective for a time, feeling the otherness of the dark man in particular, his ruthlessness like a solid rod in my solar plexus. The lighter man's running is more animal-like, and playful – just as quick but with a sense of effortlessness. It as though he only has to think about a destination in order to get there, a feeling I equate with riding an eager horse and needing only to think, *faster*, to make us both accelerate without any apparent effort. This sense of easy speed is felt most noticeably in my head and shoulders, so this becomes another anchor point for the running-men dream image.

There is yet another felt sense from the men, one stemming from their interaction with each other in the dream. The dark man suggests a destination for their chase, the upper stands of the nearby stadium where a hockey game is about to start. But there is a way that I know, as one often knows things without knowing why in dreaming, that the dark man has some kind of ill intent, that he will harm the other man in some way if he goes way up into the stadium into the section of red seats away from all the people. I hear Bosnak asking me where in particular I feel that knowing-not-to-go from the light man, and find an openness in the throat that simply says no. From this running-man dream sequence, there is a complex set of anchor points: in my solar plexus, head and shoulders, and throat. Once these are clearly felt, we move on to the other aspects of the dream, and from these I establish two more anchor points: a sense of solidness supporting my back coupled with a fluid motion in my spine that comes from an image related to my maternal grandmother. And lastly, a subtle energy surrounds my body, particularly my upper body from the felt sense of a dream image of an older woman wearing a living-green shirt made of a dream fabric with properties that do not exist in the natural world.

In the culmination of the EI practice, Bosnak asks me to sense each of the anchor points in turn and to hold them all simultaneously for a few minutes. It takes great concentration, creates an emotional intensity that makes me break out into sweat, and ends with a powerful felt sense of being lifted, and of my face filled with energy, my lips tingling. My practice is to revisit this composite for about 20 minutes a day, not necessarily in one sitting, and to keep revisiting it until the dream elements seem to lose their charge because I have absorbed them in some way, which could take days or weeks. There is no interpretation, no speculation about how this dream and its various elements relate to my life situation. But there is an expectation that if I consistently embody this powerful collection of dream elements, particularly those presences that feel most foreign to my own habitual consciousness, I will be changed in some way. Bosnak and Fischer both report many instances where dreamers are charged with creative energy, new insights or begin a healing process after working with their dreams in this way. It is a method drawn from the tenets of archetypal psychology which respects dream elements as autonomous, not as our own creations to do with as we wish. Bosnak considers us to be guests in the utterly mysterious landscape of our dreams, and as extremely privileged that whatever makes our dreams appears willing to interact with us in this way.

Jungian Approaches to Body Dreamwork

There are at least two other modern Jungian dreamwork practices that have moved beyond traditional detailed analysis and interpretation toward a more experiential and body-oriented way of being with the dream. These are Mindell's *process work*, and Aizenstat's *dream tending*. Like Bosnak, Aizenstat was deeply inspired by the ideas of Hillman and the branch of Jungian thought that became archetypal or depth psychology. Hillman (1979) said, "The golden rule in touching any dream is keeping it alive." He felt that any move we generally tend to make in working with dreams, such as projecting them into the future, relating them to the past or extracting their messages takes us away from the dream itself, and we lose its life force in exchange for our insights, a poor bargain. Hillman suggests it is better to sit with the black dog of our dream than to ascribe to it some kind of meaning such as aggression, protection or sexuality. "A living dog is better than one that is stuffed with concepts or substituted by an interpretation. For a dream image to work in life it must, like a mystery, be experienced as fully real."

Hillman moved the dream away from the realm of ego psychology, where it has lived for much of the last century, and back to its more experiential roots. He believed that the only valid way to approach dreaming is by entering into its underworld realm, subjecting ourselves to the descent, not trying to use dreams for our own purposes. He did not think we need to add anything, or compensate for what's not there. "Each dream has its own fulcrum and balance, compensates itself, is complete as it is." Hillman views any attempt to analyze, use or make sense of a dream from our logical, dayworld perspective as losing touch with the actual dreaming.

For Aizenstat (2009), working with dreams involves *tending the living image*. He suggests we have many dream figures, and that they can represent aspects of our own lives (work, relationships) or can be archetypal messengers from the collective or world unconscious. He adds another transpersonal layer above Jung's collective unconscious to encompass the entire natural world. True to Hillman, Aizenstat's dream tending advocates developing an ongoing relationship to dream figures rather than making any attempt to control, direct or question them. He saw a symbiotic relationship between us and our dream figures. If they are desolate and broken, as they mend or heal, so do we. "You are not in search of an answer, but rather an experience of what the image is revealing." One of Aizenstat's typical inquiries into dream figures is to notice their *particularity*. The bear in your dream is not just any bear, but *this* bear. "Particularity keeps us in direct, experiential contact with the dream image visiting *now*. Using our senses of touch, taste, smell, sight and hearing, we bring our instinctual body into relationship with the living image as an embodied entity." Aizenstat called this process animation of a dream image, and saw it as the way to access the deepest layer of the psyche. But he also finds the more traditional dreamwork techniques of association and amplification useful to inquire into personal, cultural and mythological aspects of the dream.

All of the embodied dreamwork methods use association as a way to begin opening up to the dream and feeling one's personal connection to it with the exception of Mindell (2000). He saw dreaming as a form of consciousness that is accessible all the time, and as more real in many ways than everyday reality. He suggested that the only reason we need to use the technique of association to figure out what our dreams mean is because we have dissociated from them in the first place. His process work is an attempt to become perpetually aware of the flow of our participation in dreaming when we are awake as well as asleep. The path to this awareness is through the body through subtle feelings, "flickering nonverbal sensations, moods and hunches."

When we dream, one of the most striking things about the experience is how very real it feels, in spite of the fact that such strange and fantastical things can take place. We have all had the experience of a dream in which something unpleasant is happening that feels so real that it takes us a few minutes upon waking to realize, with relief, that those uncomfortable images were in fact 'just a dream'. Mindell (2001) is a dream theorist who does not see the separation of waking and dreaming life as so distinct. He views dreaming as messages from the unconscious that can be found not only in nighttime dreams but also in body symptoms, daydreams, imagery and even in brief flickers of awareness that he calls *flirts*. What sets night dreams apart from waking dreamlike experiences is the relative absence of our habitual ego consciousness. In night dreams, we move further away from the fairly narrow and self-oriented way of seeing the world that excludes anything that does not fit into the set of beliefs about ourselves and the world that we have acquired during our lifetime. In night dreams, other-wordly presences have free rein, and even when our ego-self is present, it is a watered-down, less effective or central version of ourselves, just another dream character among many. Mindell (2001) pointed out the "deeply democratic" nature of what he calls the *Dreammaker*, and noted that "over time, It seems to treat all of its figures and experiences as equally important." This is one of many reasons one should not approach dreams with the same value system carried in everyday consciousness. In a dream, some of the tiniest and most seemingly-insignificant elements may turn out to be powerful catalysts.

A Focusing Approach to Dreamwork

Gendlin encouraged those working with dreams to be open and friendly with every aspect of the dream, and he seemed to take particular interest and delight in attending to the small, strange details in a dream landscape. For Gendlin, the touchstone and final authority on any dream, is the body of the person dreaming. His method of *body dreamwork* (2012) is based on *focusing* which is deeply experiential. Focusing is a way of attending inside to subtle bodily-felt sensations that continue to open and expand as one attends to them. It is reminiscent of aspects of embodied imagination, dream tending and process work. There is much overlap in all of these methods.

Gendlin saw dreams as part of the living process, but as unfinished processes that can be moved toward completion when a person works with their dreams in a particular way. He advocated allowing the images from dreams to bring a felt sense back into the body from the dream itself and to seek the places in the dream where the inherent life force is most tangible. Like all of the other embodied dreamwork practices covered here, the focusing approach allows the dream to come alive in the dreamer and to potentially change the dreamer, but not by figuring out what the dream means or even by working out how it relates to one's life situation. Gendlin suggests a person should never use a dream to make a decision because one night, a dream may seem to point in one direction, and the next night's dream might just as easily point the opposite way. Instead, he suggests the dreamer look for "the hidden positive energy [which] points to a new constellation, a change in the person, not the decision."

The Dream of the Perfect Newborn

To further illustrate focusing or body dreamwork, I will return to my personal example and pick up where the chapter began. I have left the village of Malinalco behind, and returned to the misty grey quiet of Deep Cove, back to my familiar surroundings and also to my more accustomed way of working with my dreams. *I have a disturbing dream in which I am told to perform a Caesarian even though I have no surgical training, am not even a medical student. Still I take the dream-scalpel, which has a rounded wheel of a blade, more like a glass cutter, but good in that it prevents me from cutting too deeply into the flesh of the pregnant woman. It is easier than I expect to make the incision, so I go just a little bit too far along the line drawn for me on her belly. Almost no time passes before the doctor instructing me suggests it is time to take the baby out. I reach inside the incision and pull out a tiny, perfect baby wrapped in a kind of cloth that I gently unfold like a flower. From here the dream becomes disturbing, the baby suddenly a clean, white older version that is too long and lean. The doctor is up in the bar celebrating with a drink and refuses to come back and finish the operation or instruct me further. Meanwhile, I have the alarming sense that the woman is bleeding out. I finally find someone determined to help me save her, but the young dark-haired woman who has vowed to see this problem through with me plans to do so using her computer and google searches. I am covering the wound that has become a larger gash in the woman's side, putting pressure to staunch the blood flow. At times in this frantic episode, it feels as though the woman is going to be fine, at other times as though she has lost too much blood and will not survive.*

There are many associations I can make to the various elements of the dream, and as I do this, I am aware of how parts of the dream and some of its themes bear a relationship to aspects of my life. I feel disturbed by aspects of the dream, frustrated by others, but also as though I am not really getting what it is truly about. It is only when I reenter the dream at its most-alive place that a deeply authentic sense of the dream becomes tangible. For me, the key moment is when I carefully unwrap the newborn, feel how alive and perfect it is, and begin to sense how the image lives in my own body. This is the practice of focusing. As I allow the felt sense of extracting and unwrapping the perfect newborn to come alive inside my body, I feel it in my belly in particular, and I have a different impulse than what took place in the dream. Rather than give the baby to the mother in that moment, I hold it close to my chest for a few minutes, and begin to feel the sense of a circular motion inside me, calming. The next steps in the dream – the baby changing into an older, thinner, whiter version of herself and the frantic energy of the hunt for someone to save the mother – simply fall away as though the dream itself has changed its course.

There is much I could say about how this dream relates to myself and my own birth, which was very premature and quite traumatic for both me and my mother. I am aware that I didn't get held much in those first weeks of life because I was kept in an incubator, and am sure much could be made of how this dream relates my own story. I also have a lot of associations to the pregnant woman in the dream, a woman whose history of deep trauma made the therapy work I did with her feel raw and in some ways, unfinished even after we went our separate ways. The symbolism of the still-open wound may be obvious, but the focusing approach I chose did not take me up into my head and the world of ideas and speculation about the meaning of the dream and how it relates to my personal life. No matter how brilliant such an interpretation may seem, I have learned from my own experience of working with my dreams, and the dreams of so many others, that even the best interpretation falls flat unless it resonates inside the dreamer's body. And seeking an answer that is too pat or tidily links to some aspects of the dreamer's life has a tendency to kill the aliveness of the dream image. I think of it more like interacting with a wild animal that briefly graces us with its presence, as something to savor but not to control or ask something of. Gendlin (1986) saw all dreams as friendly, as potentially leading to a growth step, and felt that by interacting with them via our body, we change into something new and we become more whole. The simple action of holding the newborn from my dream in my imagination brought a sense of this wholeness, and that seemed like enough.

However, big dreams like this one can open further, and this one did. I spent about a month revisiting the anchor points from the running-men dreamwork I did in Malinalco. It was about the time the embodied imagination process felt like it was fully cooked that I had the Caesarian dream. It was so powerful and different in character from my usual dreams that it felt like it could be a continuation of the EI process. I had the opportunity to work with Bosnak on this Caesarian dream and was invited to embody another set of anchor points based on a few of the dream's most powerful images and ending with the disturbing white baby. I had an association to the bleached bones of the bodies that were left where they died in an elementary school in Rwanda, a sight I will never forget. The association made me extremely wary of this particular dream image. What I actually found when I entered into the long-limbed pale baby was surprising – a sense of a very strong will to survive deep in the core of this living creature that now felt quite alien, but no longer in a creepy way. The best way I can describe it is the sense of what someone's body will do when hypothermic: it will pull energy away from the extremities to focus the heat on the core, on just the organs needed to keep life going. This brought a powerful sense of concentrated life force; it was such a surprise to find this life-affirming felt sense in this disturbing dream image. It seemed so much more likely that the life force would come from the first version of the baby, the perfect newborn. But dreams so often surprise us in this way that many times over, I have come to the conclusion that we should do our best to set aside our preconceptions and be open to what the actual living images in the dream bring. One of the best ways to do this is to step out of our tendency to analyze and explain, to bracket out what we think we already know and enter into a deeply embodied sense of our dreams. This allows the dreams to work on us rather than the other way around.

References

Aizenstat, S. (2009). *Dream tending*. New Orleans, LA: Spring Journal.
Gendlin, E. T. (1986). *Let your body interpret your dreams*. Wilmette, IL: Chiron Publications.

Gendlin, E. G. (2012). Body dreamwork. In D. Barrett, (Ed.). *The Encyclopedia of Sleep and Dreams*. Santa Barbara, CA: ABC-Clio.

Hillman, J. (1979). *The dream and the underworld*. New York, NY: Harper and Row Publishers.

Mindell, A. (2000). *Dreaming while awake*. Charlottesville, VA: Hampton Roads Publishing Company.

Mindell, A. (2001). *The dreammaker's apprentice*. Charlottesville, VA: Hampton Roads Publishing Company.

11 Perfect Storms
Working with Nightmares and Bad Dreams

A nightmare is the most useful dream.

Ernest Hartmann

Those who suffer from nightmares, particularly those recurrent, horrifying, trauma-based dreams that frequently tear a person from sleep by the sheer terror they generate would wonder what kind of person Hartmann was to say such a dream is useful. He did not mean such dreams are useful to the dreamer (although they can be under some circumstances). What Hartmann (1999) was referring to is how nightmares are useful to researchers of dreams. For those asking questions about the link between daily life and dreams, it can be a challenge to make such a connection if there is nothing dramatic or unusual, but rather many things going on in a person's life. With a nightmare following a major traumatic event, the link between the dream and the person's waking life becomes clear. For therapists, this link can be very helpful as well – in working with deeply frightening and unforgettable nightmares, especially those that recur, when the symptom picture begins to shift and change, it is easy to track via the changes in the client's dreams.

De-Escalating the Fear

This is one of the reasons I chose to study the effects of dreamwork treatment on the recurrent nightmares of refugees for my doctoral dissertation: if the treatment used in the study was helpful, the dreams that had plagued the study participants – in most cases repeatedly for many years – would begin to change in a way that would be obvious, not subtle. The good news is that these terrifying recurrent dreams *did* change, and in what appeared to be predictable ways. There was a pattern of de-escalation of fear response in reverse of the typical order of the nervous system's response to threat. The immobility or freeze response is the body's last-ditch effort to manage a traumatic event, and this is often the state that those with post-traumatic nightmares repeatedly experience before the terror of the dream wakes them up. After treating a small group of refugees, what I and the therapists who participated the study found was a pattern of responses that moved steadily toward more empowered reactions: from freeze to flight to fight, and a sense that the empowerment experienced in the dream stayed with them in waking life (Ellis, 2016).

After the dreamer was able to confront the aggressor in their dream, it often ceased to scare them, and the nightmare would not return again in its same form, and in some cases, not at all. This finding is not unique to my study, and in fact there are many, larger studies that support a similar way of working. The nightmares of posttraumatic stress disorder (PTSD) sufferers are not typical dreams, but tend to replicate the actual trauma event. They have been called failed dreams, or not dreams at all but flashbacks during sleep. The work with such dreams can have a helpful effect of changing the person's dreams in a way that moves them more toward typical dreams, which weave past and present and may include bizarre and/or metaphorical features. Such is the case with the dream presented here, which the client defines as a nightmare – although dream researchers define nightmares as dreams with intense negative emotion that wakes the dreamer up. Without the "waking criteria" it is merely a bad dream. However, I work with nightmares and bad dreams similarly and in clinical work, if the client defines it as a nightmare, I accept their definition.

Grateful Dead Dream Session

CLIENT: *I had a nightmare last night. In the dream I'm at work and "Jack," a man I had a history with who I don't feel safe around comes into my workplace. I know from the second I see him that he's come to kill me. I see him, in very slow motion, pulling a gun out of a brown leather holster. He starts to fire the gun, and I am somehow dodging the bullets. I know he fires 16 rounds, and I don't think he got me ... and then the dream shifts and I'm on a bus going up a mountain. It's a Grateful Dead tour bus, and it's about to make its last stop when I see Jack waiting there. I tell the bus driver if he makes the stop the man is going to get on the bus and kill me. Everyone around me urges the driver not to open the door and he doesn't, so I'm safe. We get to the top of the mountain, and as we're going back down I see Jack, and see how we've foiled his plan.*

T: Wow, that's a great dream. One thing I'm curious about is how you're feeling in the dream. It sounds like such a scary situation …

C: Yes, he lives in my town and he's a dangerous man. I went to work the other day and he was there, he knows where I work. So it makes sense I'm having this nightmare because if he were going to do something violent he would know where to find me.

T: Can you tell me a bit about the history you have with him?

C: She describes the history of emotional and verbal abuse, drug use and unpredictability. Her friends stopped to visit her, saw what was happening, and took the dreamer away from this volatile situation. "We packed up my stuff and I left with them and never looked back. But recently he moved back to my town. I had not seen him since. He didn't know I lived here but now he knows where I work. I fear becoming a target for him again."

T: So this is a very current, relevant dream. The connection to your life is clear, an expression of your worry. I'm wondering about this number 16. I wonder if anything significant happened for you at 16.

C: I lost my virginity when I was 16. That was the year I felt free for the first time. I got my license. I waited till 16 to have sex with my sweetheart. I could see myself apart from my family, had a job, was going to school, and I had a very lovely boyfriend. It was the last time my life felt idyllic and safe. All my subsequent relationships have felt unsafe and I haven't been serious with anyone. I can still remember the safety of that relationship, and since then, I have not felt that way with anyone in the context of a relationship. I can feel it somatically right now.

T: So interesting that those things are together, the 16 rounds, the feeling of being triggered, and that this was the last time you felt really safe in relationship. I'd like you to get a felt sense of that safety, with your high school sweetheart. Just immerse yourself in the feeling of that … tell me where in your body you most feel that sense of safety. Let yourself sink into this feeling of being 16 and in love with this person you feel safe with.

C: I can feel that. Like a radiating, my energetic body, my entire body feels it, I can feel a current shift in my body.

T: I can feel that too, and hear it in your voice. So that radiating current shift that is throughout your whole body, keep that with you when we go through this because it seems like a gift from the dream. Just keep going in the dream. You're on a bus now and going up a mountain, can you tell me about that?

C: It doesn't feel like an actual memory, but I have been doing research about the Grateful Dead. It was like I was on a tour with a bunch of people who were like-minded fans. That was also something that made me a possible target, him knowing what my interests are. But the people on the bus were really loving and supportive. I don't know any of them, but in the dream I did. And I felt really safe.

T: So there's the concern of being tracked, and the not knowing. The feeling I would like you to pick up on is this feeling of like-minded people and the sense of community around the Grateful Dead, which is interesting considering you have just been shot at. Because it feels like it could be a joke in your dream,

a bit of dream humour (laughter). It also seems to be about this camaraderie and safety, and the dream bringing this to you in a few ways: the like-minded people and being safe. Feel that?
C: I do, I really do.
T: Then you see Jack at the last stop and know if he gets on the bus he'll kill you … but he doesn't.
C: Yeah, nobody lets that happen.
T: You have the driver and the Grateful Dead fans all really being protective and keeping you safe.
C: What do you think about the bus?
T: Vehicles can be metaphors for relationship. So the bus could potentially be a metaphor for your relationship with groups. I don't usually like to take direct advice from dreams but something in this might be saying you could surround yourself with like-minded people. I don't know how this is in your life right now. Setting Jack aside – which is a current situation that's very real and I don't want to minimize it – this could be a dream about going from isolation to being in community and finding safety in that. Or returning to the feeling of that love relationship from high school where a sense of safety was very much a given. This dream could be commenting on your relationship situation and asking you to find your people.
C: That's what I want to do.
T: You can actually follow this feeling, the one you have with you that's bringing you a sense of safety, reminding you where to find it.
C: What the 16 shots do is reunite me with the sense of community, they get me to shift into a place that is supportive and nurturing of me and not destructive.
T: Yes, that's right where the dream does this dramatic scene shift. And you don't think he gets you – he shoots at you 16 times but misses, like the classic action movie where they shoot the hero and never seem to actually hit the target. And then again, he may have succeeded, in the logic of this dream, a way you're grateful for this death, which isn't literal, but you are in the Grateful Dead bus. It's like, oh good, that's done. That could be another way to read it that shifts you… it seems like it just happens, an abrupt shift. One thing I might suggest is to say more about the end here, where he doesn't get on the bus, but you see him there as you drive back down…
C: He was waiting for the bus to make this stop, but when the bus didn't stop, it threw a kink in his plan. He was wearing a Grateful Dead shirt. He was trying to seem like one of us. We were protected by the bus. So maybe it's like my community or how I'm trying to shift into a feeling of safety. There is something in there about the false impressions I have of people before I get to know them. Especially with Jack, I had very wrong impressions of him, and that's happened in the last couple of relationships I've been in where the guy seems like one thing at the beginning but then… I have to look beyond the façade.
T: So maybe to help you with that, if you feel ok to try this, just imagine into Jack, that version of him on the side of the road, where his plans have been foiled because the bus didn't stop for him and just to get a feeling into the

character of the dream Jack, not the actual one. Just notice how that is held in your body. (pause) We won't stay long because I can see it's not comfortable, but what can you tell me from there?

C: There's like a hollowness, where it feels really cloudy and like I could vomit. There's this murky ... I almost feel dizzy right now. Wherever that character is, it's sick.

T: It's sick, feels empty ... so just step outside of that, you can leave it behind, I just wanted you to sample it. And then put yourself back in the end of the dream where you're on the bus going back down the hill, leaving him behind, you see him on the side there, and just let the dream play forward from there, where you're on the bus with your allies and friends and leaving Jack there on the side of the road.

C: I can feel the release of the tension I've been holding. Like I don't have to worry about him anymore. I can really be present.

T: So if the release is like a breath, draw it out longer, really feel that release. Just let your whole body exhale and let the tension go until it's all drained away. Take some time with it.

C: (long silence) It feels good.

T: This feels like a natural stopping place – does it feel okay to leave it here?

C: (assent, pause). I can't believe the analogies you were able to draw. That's what's so exciting about dreamwork, just getting another perspective and then seeing it, thinking oh my god, of course. It's hard to do on your own.

T: Most of us have a blind spot with own dreams. I know I do. With a dream like this, it is partly symbolic and there's a lot in it outside of your life situation. But with your life situation and Jack, it's hard to set that aside. I can see how all that you would see in this dream is what you *already* see; it's too hard to step outside of it. But I'm not in your life so it's easier for me. I can see all the other things. I actually see this as a very hopeful dream. Usually a nightmare will not have that last part – they usually stop earlier, right in the scariest place. I often get people to dream the dream on to get to a safer place. But your dream continues on to a place where you *are* safe and it's basically showing you that when you are in the company of other like-minded people, you are safe. I'm reminded of when you were with Jack, and your friends came and took you away. It's a clear example of how your friends keep you safe. It may be underscoring that part and helping you feel into the places in your past where you have been safe as well. It feels like gift, not just to show you the situation but also the way out of it.

C: Yes I see that now. I feel much better having moved through all that.

In a follow-up session two weeks later, the client said that the dreamwork had taken the charge out of her life situation, and out of her body. The sense of feeling safer had stayed with her. She had a follow-up dream about Jack a week later. *While she was talking to a friend about the difficult times she had when she was with him, he approached her and started to yell at her. In her dream, she said, "You can't yell at me for talking through this experience, it's my right." He agreed and said he was sorry.* She had not been triggered since the dreamwork, and in her subsequent dream she was able to stand up to the man she had been so afraid of, and he apologized. The following is an excerpt of the follow-up conversation:

T: Could you say a little bit about how the nightmare dreamwork has evolved?
C: Prior to working that dream I felt really anxious. The dream had taken place at my work, and because I had seen him at my job, there was fear entering into that space. After the dreamwork, the fear had really dissipated. There was a shift where I wasn't worried or afraid. I didn't hurry walking into the door. I'm not afraid if he walks by or if he comes in. I'm not holding a charge anymore. And then having the dream the other night where he appeared, I was nervous in the dream at first. But I stood up to him and then he backed off and apologized and that re-dissipated the charge. The work we did strengthened the part of me that feels like I can stand up to him and confront him, or anyone. I feel better supported too. The part of the dream about the bus and support of community was really helpful too.

Finding Help as a Form of Resourcing

This progression toward less fear and greater empowerment within the dream and in waking life is common to many forms of nightmare dreamwork. What I concluded after an intensive study of nightmares is that there is a strong link between physiological activation and the nature of a person's dreams. People with an anxious temperament, or those whose nervous systems can't settle after trauma, will have dreams that reflect this base-level anxiety. If one of the functions of dreaming is to dissipate emotional charge, then it makes sense that those whose bodies are carrying a lot of fear will have nightmares, which can be seen as the body's attempt to bring up and dissipate the fear. The problem is that the physiological fear response can be so intense, it wakes the dreamer up right in the scariest place in the dream. Then the dream can't do its job, and in fact it has the opposite of the desired effect because it disrupts sleep and stirs up fear without resolving it. This is where the idea of dreaming the dream forward can be so helpful. This idea originates with Jung, but has been picked up by numerous other dreamwork methods. In the above example, had the dream stopped at the place where the client was being shot at, I would have suggested she dream the dream forward from there. In this case, however, the dream itself shifted and carried the dreamer forward to a place of safety in the company of like-minded people. Much of what I was doing in the beginning of the session was helping the dreamer to locate and embody the sense of safety, using the resource the dream was providing because from there, exploring the aggressor in the dream, and dreaming the dream forward seemed to be more likely to be constructive.

There are a variety of ways to approach the creation of a new dream ending, and the choice depends on both the therapist's philosophical approach, as well as the nature of the client and their trauma-related dreams. My Jungian-oriented, and client-centered leanings incline me to suggest the dreamer enter into the dreamscape as fully as possible to let the dream continue in a way that resembles actual dreaming, where the dreamer does not control the content directly but allows it to unfold. There is some evidence that the process works better when the new dream direction is left open, rather than changed to something positive. Krakow and Zadra (2006) speculated that the open-ended instruction "leaves open a psychological window through which the patient may intuitively glimpse multilayered solutions to other emotional conflicts." I think the new dream ending must feel authentic to be deeply experienced, and to move the business of the dream forward in the direction it was intended to go. An ending that's surprising is an indication of the authenticity of the process.

Working with PTSD Nightmares

Other methods may involve more direct participation of the dreamer, asking what they would like to have happen. A modified version of this process, called Imagery Rehearsal Therapy (IRT), asks the dreamer to use a similar process with any dream, not necessarily their nightmare, and to change the dream in any way they want to. They are then asked to repeatedly rehearse the new ending. In several studies, IRT has been shown to significantly reduce the symptoms of PTSD (e.g., Krakow, Hollifield, et al., 2001; Krakow et al., 2000). On the strength of this evidence the American Academy of Sleep Medicine recommends IRT as the main non-pharmaceutical intervention for the treatment of PTSD nightmares. IRT is not the first nor the only nightmare treatment that invites dreamers to enter and alter their frightening dreams, but it is the method that has amassed the strongest evidence base.

I had been using Jung's idea of dreaming the dream onward for many years, and discovered IRT as I was doing the literature review for my nightmare study. It was encouraging to find such relevant and supportive evidence, and in my study, I attempted to advance the understanding of what was happening in the process of revisiting and allowing nightmares to continue. I inquired into exactly how PTSD nightmares change, how specific symptoms are affected, and what might be the mechanism of action. My original intention was to conduct quantitative research with refugees who had been referred to the Vancouver Association for the Survivors of Torture (VAST) for help with their trauma. The clinical director, Mariana Martinez-Vieyra, told me that nightmares were the single most challenging symptom for her clients, and she was willing to collaborate with me on a study to see if working with their dreams could reduce their symptoms.

Unexpectedly, a few months into the study, after training the therapists, recruiting participants and completing just a few of the cases, the Canadian federal government withdrew the funding they had been providing to VAST. It was so disappointing that this wonderful little agency that had been operating mostly with volunteers for 25 years was forced to close its doors. My study was also one of the casualties. Fortunately, I had recorded all the sessions that had been completed and had many hours of session transcripts, enough data for a qualitative study of the course of treatment for five of the participants. The data included progressive dream series and enough information to inquire into how these nightmares changed as a result of experientially re-entering and allowing the dreams to continue.

The results of the study were published in *Dreaming* (Ellis, 2016). To implement the study, I developed an abbreviated focusing-oriented dreamwork treatment protocol that included safety measures and ways to empower and resource clients as they worked with their recurring nightmares. My sense is that working directly with the nightmares was effective because I viewed these dreams as the body's repeated attempts to revisit and come to terms with the trauma that the dreams depicted. I found that after treatment, the participants' dreams, which had been largely unchanging, began to shift in specific ways: the identity of the dream aggressor started to shift to become less like the aggressor in the original trauma. The dream ego (or the "I" in the dream) became progressively more empowered, moving forward on a continuum from freeze to flight to fight as dreamers began to speak up, ask for help and/or take action. Temporal and setting changes generally shifted from being stuck in the exact time and place of the trauma to weave in elements from current life. This reflects more normal dreaming and the memory consolidation processes which seem to be inherent in effective dreams. As the dreamers became more empowered in their dreams, they woke up less afraid and there was a positive effect on daytime functioning. On average, post-traumatic stress symptoms, especially re-experiencing and avoidance symptoms, were reduced by half.

What is it that causes this helpful effect? It had not occurred to the dreamers in my study to manipulate their dream imagery, but doing so was generally empowering for them. It gave them a constructive action they could take when they awoke from a nightmare and subsequently, in their actual dreaming, they seemed to be more inclined to seize the same kind of power. The more empowered the response is, the less frightening and the more healing the dream is likely to be, and the less likely it is to recur. Such activity might be construed as a form of dream training similar to the way lucid dreamers develop dreaming skills to cultivate consciousness awareness and/or control of their dreaming. The difference in lucid dreaming is that the new dream ending happens within the dream rather than afterward – and this also has been shown to be effective for working with nightmares.

Exposure and Mastery: Proposed Mechanisms of Action

A thorough review of the mechanisms of action in nightmare therapy, resulting in reduced nightmare frequency and distress, favors dreamwork while awake. Rousseau and Belleville (2018) reviewed all studies of nightmare treatment using dreamwork, and also conducted a thematic analysis to determine the mechanisms of action most commonly cited. They found that an increased sense of mastery was the most popular hypothesis, but proposed that the main mechanism of action is more likely exposure to the fear, followed by incorporation of incompatible dream elements while awake, and then in dreaming. This process then leads to an increased sense of mastery, and reduced arousal and avoidance. They suggest clinicians should target mastery, change in beliefs around nightmares, and decreasing arousal and avoidance in treating recurrent PTSD nightmares.

My conclusions, although based on a much smaller sample, are similar. I found that increased control and empowerment, first while working with the dream in the waking state, and then while dreaming, can stop the cycle of fear for PTSD sufferers. If a person can remain calm enough to complete the dream while awake, this may translate into the ability to remain calm enough in the dreaming state itself so that they are not startled awake, and their dream can finish. The dreamer could (and some did) also take the ability to calm themselves from their dreaming into their waking life either working with the nightmares that do still occur or working with other difficult daytime situations. They tend to sleep better, be less afraid to fall asleep, and more able to calm themselves, if needed, upon wakening. These are the kinds of changes that occurred, to varying degrees, with the participants in my study. One of the participants described how the process helped him to gain power over his nightmares: "I have control on the dream, not the dream on me."

References

Ellis, L. (2016). Qualitative changes in recurrent PTSD nightmares after focusing-oriented dreamwork. *Dreaming*, 26(3), 185–201.

Hartmann, E. (1999). The nightmare is the most useful dream. *Sleep and hypnosis*, 1(4), 199–203.

Krakow, B., Hollifield, M., Schrader, R., Koss, M., Tandberg, D., Lauriello, J., & McBride, L. (2000). A controlled study of imagery rehearsal for chronic nightmares in sexual assault survivors with PTSD: A preliminary report. *Journal of Traumatic Stress*, 13(4), 589–609.

Krakow, B., Hollifield, M., Johnston, L., Koss, M., Schrader, R., Warner, T. D… Prince, H. (2001). Imagery rehearsal therapy for chronic nightmares in sexual assault survivors with posttraumatic stress disorder: a randomized controlled trial. *JAMA*, 286, 537–545.

Krakow, B., & Zadra, A. (2006). Clinical management of chronic nightmares: Imagery rehearsal therapy. *Behavioral Sleep Medicine*, 4(1), 45–70.

Rousseau, A., & Belleville, G. (2018). The mechanisms of action underlying the efficacy of psychological nightmare treatments: A systematic review and thematic analysis of discussed hypotheses. *Sleep Medicine Reviews*, 39, 122–133.

12 Fellow Travelers

Working with Dreams in Groups

A bit of our soul is exposed when sharing a dream with others.

Montague Ullman

Ullman (1996/2006) developed what is arguably the most well-known dream group method. He called it a way of *appreciating* dreams rather than interpreting them. His aim was to create a safe method for anyone to work with dreams in a group whether or not you were trained as a dream analyst. Ullman's method originated as a way to teach dreamwork to students of psychotherapy, but what he found along the way was that the dream group process can widen and enrich dreamwork, opening avenues of insight and exploration that might not come up in the traditional one-on-one therapy setting.

For those interested in pursuing group dreamwork as a way of practicing, there are more detailed accounts available of how dream groups can be structured than I have the space to cover here. The best way to learn is to join or start a dream group yourself, and it can help to have at least one person familiar with the process to keep the group on track until that part becomes seamless.

The two most prevalent ways to work with dreams in groups were developed by Ullman and Taylor (2001), and both are transparent in their use of projections by group member as a key part of the dreamwork process. I have found these methods useful in teaching dreamwork because the group process can so effectively demonstrate the incredible depth and richness that can come from even the briefest of dream images. The process also teaches members exactly how it feels to project one's own material onto someone else's dream. It makes what we all tend to do automatically more deliberate. With such practice and experience, projection becomes a conscious choice for the dreamworker, and opinions about whether or not one should offer these is sharply divided.

Taylor's Projective Dreamwork

Jeremy Taylor clearly loved the process of offering projections. His group method is simpler than Ullman's, and includes his own clearly-articulated set of beliefs about the nature of dreams and dreamwork. Taylor's method is so embracing of the process of group projection that it is named "projective dreamwork." I once spent a long weekend in a marathon dream group session with Taylor; about 20 of us spent many hours, late into the evening, offering all of our projections regarding each and every person's dream, with Jeremy typically offering the closing remarks with vigor and a sense of humor. I can still picture Jeremy saying, "As the night gets later, the projections get wilder, and wilder …" as a preface to his own offering of his projections onto the dream. The beauty of offering these statements as if they are the participants' dream is that it leaves the dreamer free to accept what resonates and discard what does not. The down-side is that many hours can be spent on aspects of the dream that don't resonate with the dreamer, and so can dilute the process or send it off on tangents not deeply relevant to the dreamer and their dream. My preference is for one-on-one dreamwork with a person over time, so deep trust can develop and patterns of dreaming emerge. I use group dreamwork mainly to teach, but can also see how rich the process can get when groups work together over time. The dreams provide a way for people to connect at a much deeper level than they would otherwise, and sometimes over many years.

Another form of dream group process called person-centered approach group incident process (PCAGIP) was pioneered in Japan. The method was initially developed by Shoji Murayama (2015), a former student of Carl Rogers, who sought a way to make group case consultations feel safer for the presenter. The method is democratic, no criticism is permitted, and there is no requirement to reach a conclusion; rather the goal is to create a pool of potential ideas about how to intervene. Tsutsui (2018) adapted PCAGIP to facilitate group dreamwork and offered a case example of a dream of pregnancy presented by a graduate student in her twenties. *In the dream, she thought she was pregnant and felt heavy in her abdomen. Although she was pleased, she thought she could neither give birth, given* her current situation as a student, nor could she abort. As she was thinking about what to do, she woke up.

In one of the early phases of PCAGIP, each group member takes a turn, in order, asking a question about the dream. Then members take turns offering impressions, thoughts and associations, and in a further step each member invites the dreamer into some form of experiencing of their dream. For example, a group member asked, "If you talk to the heaviness, how would it answer?" The dreamer noticed that she needed to tend aspects of herself that were hidden from the light of day, and to improve "ventilation" of her feelings "so that heaviness can open its eyes." Further inquiry into this ventilation brought the word "patience" to the dreamer. In following up a week later, the dreamer said she had gained a sense of security in the knowledge that she would be okay no matter what happened in the future.

The Lion Dream Session: An Ullman Group Process

The following is a script of an Ullman dream group process that provides specific detail about how such a process might unfold. This session was used as a vehicle for teaching, so there are a few places where I abandon the Ullman method and to explore alternative ways I might work with such a dream. This would not happen in a more classic Ullman group where there is no leader, and all members are considered equal. A notable instance in the following example of where I depart from the Ullman protocol is when the dreamer becomes shaky. I feel compelled to tell her she need not identify with the dream ego (about to be killed), though this feels more directive than what I would normally offer. The assumption that we are equivalent to the 'I' in the dream is a common one, but I tend to favor the view from archetypal psychology that the dream ego is another dream character, albeit one with qualities that may directly reflect the dreamer's. Fortunately, the direction I guided the process did resonate with the dreamer. This session ends with a good example of the popular experiential practice of 'being a dream element.'

I am on a horse and it's slowly clip-clopping down a street in the suburbs. It's very quiet, I don't see any cars or people around. I look behind me and see this huge lion is following me. A heavy fear/dread comes over me. I have a sense that even if I gallop, the lion will be faster and catch me. The horse morphs into a bicycle, and there is a sense the dream is trying to help me, that maybe a bike will be faster. But again I am so slow. Each pedal round is slow and labored like I am going up a steep hill (but I'm not). I can't seem to go any faster and the lion is still following. I decide to turn down an even quieter street. On the smaller street, there are no cars or people either. It feels eerily empty. However, there is one house just near me where I see a man holding his front door slightly open. I throw the bike down by the shrubs in his front yard and rush into this open door, and the man lets me in. In that instant, I get a huge sense that he is a harmful person and that he wants to hurt me (i.e. rapist or murderer). I immediately re-open the front door wide, but hide behind it and let the lion come in. Then I race outside and leave the lion in the house with the man. I walk back onto the road and look around. I see from all directions there are other lions coming toward me. There are at least four or five of them. I feel I have to give up. There is nothing more I can do.

First the group asks clarifying questions, which are strictly confined to making sure we all understand the details of the dream itself. The transcript below picks up at the Ullman stage of offering personal projections, but because my theoretical orientation involves focusing, I do this step in a focusing-oriented way. I ask the participants in our group to take some time to enter into the dream, embody it, use as many senses as possible and then speak about the dream from their own felt sense of it. This differs from the classic Ullman method where dreamers' comments are prefaced with, "If this were my dream …" I have found that even with the "my dream" preface, some dream group participants find a way to offer advice or comment to the dreamer directly, whereas when they are invited to find their own felt sense of the dream, no such confusion arises.

PARTICIPANT 1: I am entering the dream and see the lion. I look at his eyes and they are telling me what are you going to do now? I feel that the only thing I can do is surrender. I surrender, and that's the way I escape. But at the same time it's not just to have a feeling it's okay, they are going to eat me, it's more of a sensation that they are inviting me to do something I haven't done yet.

P2: I was so relieved to wake up from this. I was wondering, maybe escape is possible, I just haven't considered the options. And at the same time this very real sense that actually there isn't a way to escape. And that's why I felt relieved that it stopped. Things felt very heavy.

P3: I had a felt sense of the quiet. I could feel that there are no helpers here. Initially some frustration, why is the horse/bike so slow, why does that man have to be unsafe? And then yearning for more help, and then later I kind of just got quiet. And also I found myself, part quiet, yet the other part thought of escape routes – can't climb, lions can climb… so maybe I haven't quite gotten to that acceptance.

T: I am also entering this dream, and I can feel how quiet it is, for me eerily quiet, sterile … like in the movie *Blue Velvet* where there is a perfect ordinary looking sweet town, but there's this undercurrent of creepiness. It has this feeling of, looks like a nice place, but there's nobody home, it's quiet, there's a disconnection. I'm not connected to this horse even, where I'd usually be feeling, 'nice pony.' It feels like there is some kind of human element missing. There's no kids playing on the street… of course there are lions everywhere, so who would let their kids out? And also, hold on, I feel like I've done this great thing, I've got the lion in with this bad man and closed the door, and then shit! There are so many more lions out there, it feels like it's not fair, it's playing with my emotions like a horror movie.

As the keeper of the process steps (a role that anyone can pick up once all are familiar with the steps), I suggest we all check in on our sense of the dream one more time to see if there's more. This part of the process can go on for a long time, especially if there are many group members. Once it feels complete (or complete enough if time is limited) the floor is turned back over to the dreamer to see if she has a response.

DREAMER: Huge. It was huge what you said. There was this moment where I was transfixed by what you said because it made so much sense. I feel shaky and weak, I had this huge wave of something, and I still feel it. I'm shaking, look at me. It made me turn around and look at the lion for the first time, and he is gold, magnificent, powerful and huge. And he's frightening and I am so insignificant. And this feeling of, what do you want and he's telling me he wants to consume me, completely ... I will be consumed by this. He is so much bigger than me and I am fighting, trying to find the way out and I'm fighting him and yet it is inevitable. The heaviness, I am me right now, but when I am in him, I will be powerful, light and big. But insignificant me is looking for an escape. And this personal will that I think is my protection is completely misguided ... to think that this little house I can go in will keep me safe and that this little body is going to be enough, and it's like, who am I kidding? I have a sense of, just give up and take the invitation.

I shift from away this feeling that I am something and can get away from this power, to sense that as so ridiculous actually. Just give in, just stop this whole ridiculous fight because what is waiting is actually quite magnificent. But there is a part of me that is afraid of dying. So it's a very spiritual dream in a sense, it's about spirituality and it feels like I'm afraid of that. All I have to do is let go, and I am in the place of being afraid to let go. And it's very personal, that's why there's nobody around. It feels like my journey, there is no one else involved. There's a misguided feel to it. I think this, I think that... but am wrong. Just looking at the lion changed it all. It's huge and magnificent and wants to just consume me. I will have to die.

T: I know this is kind of out of step with the method but I do feel like I want to say to you that the 'I' is the dream ego. It's the you in the dream, but not equivalent to you. These kinds of dreams, at least at one level, are speaking about ego death. The ego is afraid to lose its primacy. But what's happening is that you're becoming part of something much larger and the ego is terrified of course. I'm just saying that because you're shaky, and I want to say that maybe the fear is coming from the small "s" self, because everything fights for its life. I don't know if it helps to hear that?

D: Yes it does because in the dream the small self is struggling, fighting, trying to find a way, a tree I can climb. And the house and the man represented a misguided idea that this was going to help. Yes that makes a lot of sense, that the "I" is the ego.

T: I think it's an important point to say: that there is a dream ego that we tend to conflate with ourselves, but it's not. It's the image of oneself in the dream, and it can be seen to represent our ego. This dream makes it feel to the dream ego like life is over, but in the grand scheme of things, in a dream like this which is so spiritual, it's what all of the people who meditate every day are trying to have happen, this death of the ego, or at least relativizing of it. So I just felt the need to say that.

D: It totally makes sense and it feels right.

We move on to check the context and I ask if there was anything happening in her life at the time of this dream that seems relevant.

D: I have been doing this kind of work for a very long time, it's my main focus in life. That's my passion, to keep growing, that's what I do. This is directly … such a huge … I can't describe how I feel to get that this is what its message was. I feel so in awe of it, that a dream like that came to show me again to contemplate the letting go because that's something that I battle constantly. My identity as a therapist, for example, which I know gets in the way of my spiritual work sometimes, so it's a constant feeling of letting go. What am I clinging to right now? There's a part of me fighting for survival and it's so lovely to have that come up and say, ok, look at this lion. It is explaining my fears a bit and putting them into this context for me.

T: So, it's a really big dream.

D: I feel really grateful for it actually. I feel really touched by it. It's like there is a sense of help given here to have a dream that puts it into this context.

T: I am abandoning this (Ullman group) process again … but I'm wondering if you could just imagine being the lion. Just see him, see his size and his golden color and his power, and feel what part of his body you feel you could enter, maybe his shoulders, or the walking… just whatever feels like something that could help you slip into his perspective, his essence … (silence)

D: He's pretty amazing … (silence). There is an expansion, an opening that happens … (more silence).

T: An opening …

D: There's a place you go to when you're meditating, where you expand, it's that feeling. I won't stay here because you just disappear when you're that lion… but he… I can feel a wanting, a yearning to the human, he wants to merge but not merge because he's way bigger. Consume is probably a better word.

T: You're feeling into his relationship to …

D: … that little person on the bike. It's not like he's a kind and gentle lion; he's not a reassuring nice lion. He's like, you're done … he doesn't have opinions and judgements and things like that, he just is. It is what it is, you're done, I am just going to take you.

T: Yeah, very impersonal

D: Yeah, he's not dark, he's bright and light, expansive, huge. And quite magnificent. What a grand lion. It feels nice being the lion… Oh wow, that was great.

T: We will kind of go back through the dream and I'll just read the steps. What might happen though, my sense is that it might feel different. I don't quite know how to put this … a dream is like snapshot of where we are and I have a feeling that you're not there anymore and I don't know if the dream will feel the same. So when I read it, instead of feeling like you have to be true to the original dream … if there is something different, or it changes in any way, feel free to let it. Don't feel it has to be accurately remembered if you know what I mean, but more accurate to how you are living with this dream now. So …

I'm on a horse and it's slowly clopping down the street in the suburbs. It's a blue-sky day and it's quiet and calm. I don't see any cars and people around, and I turn around and see this huge lion following me... feel back into the scene and notice what's there, and if anything has shifted.

D: Totally. There's no more fear. That heaviness in the dream is not there, and I feel now as though I am looking at this person from the lion's perspective. And so it just becomes a scene I'm watching. I am no longer in that bike person. And it's like, I don't feel the dread. The dread is gone, the heaviness is gone.

T: So you're no longer identified with the person on the bike and you don't feel the fear because the fear was in that dream character...?

D: I'm actually following the person from the lion's perspective and am like, ah, there's a little bit of humour involved. Now the lion's got feelings, great... there's a little bit of affection. Seeing this little person on the bike trying to pedal away (laughter), that's all right, you go ahead, sure, go in the house... sort of like bemusement at a child. So cute you're trying to do that. There's a nice contentment right now of a parent watching her child trying all these things out... not going to work, there's a bad man in there.

T: So, actually we don't need to go through the dream scene by scene, it's very different.

D: It feels like it's going to continue to work. There's a lot of energy doing its thing right now (gesturing toward her body). It will take some time...

T: Like it's recalibrating or something...

D: It's like this feeling inside my body right now, wow that's so powerful. And everything you all said made sense, all your comments made sense – the heaviness, wanting to escape, everything you said clicked.

T: Okay maybe we can now just do a round and pick up from the Ullman process and speak to our sense of the gift this dream is bringing. Some of this is pretty darn obvious now but, just check in and see if any of you have anything you want to offer to the dreamer based on all that's happened... (silence)

P1: The dream offers an example of going and finding the resource inside instead of trying to find something from the outside. The surrender part, I think it offers a way out of the situation.

T: To follow on from that, what I feel is like, wow, there is so much of a difference in how a scene like this is perceived depending on what perspective you are coming from. The perspective is so different if you are the lion than if you are the person on the bike, or the watcher that sees it all... that changes everything. I think of it as a something for myself to remember too, that the feel of a situation can be so different depending on your vantage point. It feels like quite a profound thing actually.

P3: Back to that little girl. She was looking for help from outside. When I became the adult facing the fear, that was a gift to me. Just look the lion in the eye and that's when all the richness came. Rather than just run, it's like facing the fear, that was the key.

T: And the dreamer gets the last word...

D: What was really interesting is that when you were all talking (at the beginning of the process), there was a moment where there was a sense of a tower that just collapsed. Because of what all of you said, it suddenly clicked this dream into place for me. I could feel a dissolution that happened, and the energy that started to move. It was quite amazing, this dissolution. I was honestly so … oh my god, it just cracked, so much just got moved, and it's all here at the moment, but yeah, that was incredible to have that feeling as your words started to hit all the right spots.

The Dreamer's Reflections

In the Ullman group process, the dreamer would offer follow-up thoughts at the start of the next group meeting before the group moved on to another dream, typically the most recent and pressing dream. Here are some of the dreamer's follow-up thoughts about the lion dream.

The scene with the man in the house feels like it is the mind fooling the me into thinking the house is a safe place to seek refuge. However, the mind is also capable of self-torture. That is, if the man is my mind, he/it is going to torture me. This is something I have struggled with a lot this year, dealing with a relentless and brutal inner critic. When I trick the man into letting the lion into the house, it feels this speaks to a tendency to try and outsmart the mind and give higher me what I think she needs. I try to let go of being attached to things, like wanting to be a good therapist. And then I feel quite satisfied because I think I've reached a new level in my growth. I'm working it too hard! I know that giving up my work is not necessarily needed but I feel like I have to not want it in order to be in it in a different way. So I fool myself around that because deep down I am still attached. I think the dream is highlighting the ridiculousness of this premise. It's telling me, forget this silly plotting, there is only one way to be free: allow the lion to consume you.

The lion is bright, gold and powerful. He is in stark contrast to my previous slow and ineffectual methods of moving through the dream world. My body tells me clearly that there is actually only one lion. He is pure consciousness that wants to consume the human aspect so I can live life as a free, awakened being. The lion is huge compared with the slow dream-human who is laboring away. My fear of letting go causes me to look for safety in the human perspective. But I end up unsafe and trapped. In the end, I just need to simply surrender, to stop running from it and stop working so hard at it because this awakening is inevitable.

The dream feels like a confirmation of my journey and it also offers guidance. It is telling me, yes, this is what you are up to in life and it's good. The dream gives me an image for the fear I feel and an image that symbolizes "working too hard." It's easier to face this (as yet unformed) concept of identity death when I have a solid image and story. It gives me permission to be afraid and reveals that controlling the process won't achieve anything. These symbols are very reassuring. This journey of self-discovery is something I am consciously doing in life. About a week before this dream I listened to a talk called "redefining death" which described letting go of identity as "the death before death." It framed letting go as comparable to an actual death experience. Something clicked for me after that talk, and then a few days later I had this dream.

This final comment by the dreamer makes me feel better about offering the idea of the dream as being potentially about ego death. This is an interpretation nevertheless, and something to be offered tentatively. I worry that my position as group leader lends my comments too much weight and see this as a danger of the projective dreamwork process. In dyadic dreamwork, I am much more circumspect with my interpretations, and in any case, as Ullman suggests, the dreamer always has the last word.

References

Hikasa, M., Kosaka, Y. & Murayama, S. (2015). Person Centered Approach Group Incident Process (PCAGIP): A New Presenter-Friendly Approach to Case Conference. *The Folio*, 26.

Taylor, J. (2001). Group work with dreams: The "Royal Road" to meaning. In K. Bulkeley (Ed.), *Dreams: A reader on religious, cultural and psychological dimensions of dreaming*. New York, NY: Palgrave, pp. 195–208.

Tsutsui, Y. (2018): How the Meaning of Dreams Emerge in PCAGIP Dreamwork: An investigation from a dream of pregnancy [In Japanese], *Japanese Journal of Humanistic Psychology*, 36, 21–31.

Ullman, M. (1996/2006). *Appreciating dreams: a group approach*. New York, NY: Cosimo-on-Demand.

13 How Dreams Enlarge Us
Big Dreams

When you were a wandering desire in the mist, I too was there, a wandering desire. Then we sought one another, and out of our eagerness dreams were born. And dreams were time limitless, and dreams were space without measure.

Kahlil Gibran

Jung coined the phrase "big dreams" to describe dreams so qualitatively different from our typical everyday dreams they deserve their own category. Defining characteristics include closer resemblance to visions than typical dreams, a consistent, purposeful structure (versus the meandering and sudden shifts in more typical dreams) and a meaning that is very clear. Jung would say such dreams are archetypal in nature because they speak to universal human patterns and seem to come from a wider collective unconscious rather than a purely personal origin. While some would say all dreams have this transpersonal dimension, big dreams transport us immediately into our relationship with something larger than ourselves. Working with such dreams has the potential to change the dreamer's life trajectory, and to prepare them for the ultimate transformation at the end of life.

122 *How Dreams Enlarge Us*

This chapter provides examples of both a big dream, and a dream that prepares the dreamer for death.

Many researchers and writers have weighed in on this topic. The International Association for the Study of Dreams launched a project to gather such dreams and compile them in the book, *Dreams that Change Our Lives*. Bulkeley (2016) wrote a book entitled, *Big Dreams* that explored the topic, in particular how such dreams awaken the dreamer to a spiritual dimension and are "a primal wellspring of religious experience." Kuiken's *impactful* dreams (e.g., Kuiken and Sikora, 1993) could also be considered big dreams. However, none of these books or studies describe in detail how one might work clinically with such a dream. It is clearly true of these dreams that they have the potential to change us whether we spend time exploring them in therapy or not. However, their impact can be greatly enhanced if they are explored and considered deeply, and such dreams can be revisited many times over the course of life.

The following is an example of such a dream that was generously shared by a woman who worked with me on this dream a decade after it occurred. This abridged transcript of our 90-minute conversation shows that working with such dreams is invaluable even many years after the fact. Also, because such a dream is more vivid and transparent than usual, the dreamwork can take more of the form of a conversation or mutual exploration that is as much directed by the dreamer as the therapist.

The Honoré Women Dream Session

A woman in her 40s with dark hair and a serene face is preparing for a journey. She travels far into the rugged wilderness (possibly Canada). She is looking for something. She comes across a high grey/brown rock face full of nooks and crannies, walks past, then suddenly stops and walks back a few steps. Then she sees her: an ancient woman sitting against the rock face. Her whole body and face is the colour and texture of the rock. She blends in so completely, you could easily walk past and not see her. The young woman has found who she is looking for.

The old woman holds out her hand and the young woman puts her hand inside. I can hear the thoughts in the old woman's head: she believes the young woman is not the one, because she is still too young, has not experienced enough and most importantly, has never borne children. However they continue to hold hands, the old woman reading and feeling the entire history of the young woman: she IS the one. She communicates (telepathically) to the younger woman that her training will begin.

The scene shifts to the young woman in a grassy field next to the mountains dancing and singing with happiness. During the training the young woman lives in a rickety wooden hut. The old woman lives outside; her body is of a vibration that doesn't need what a normal physical body would need to survive. The training is transmitted telepathically via the old woman's hands.

Many years seem to pass and when I next see the young woman she looks much older, perhaps 80 or 90. The old woman knows her time is nearly at an end. The training is done. The old woman bids farewell and goes into the field by the mountains. It is autumn, the colours all gold and brown. The old woman stands in the middle of a field and as a wind comes blowing through, the woman's body disintegrates into pieces that look like autumn leaves which are carried away by the wind.

We can now call the woman who is left behind the old woman. She packs some small supplies from the hut and journeys back out of the wilderness. Somehow I know the old hut falls apart and is absorbed back into the forest. The woman travels many days out of the wilderness back to civilization, a small town. She hires about five of the local carpenters and leads them into the wilderness, a journey of many days. At last they come to a place deep in the forest, and she instructs the men to build a wooden hut. The woman goes through the forest and picks out fallen trees as she prefers not to cut down living trees. When the hut is complete, the woman pays the men and tells them they can leave and must never mention this place to anyone nor ever return.

The men try to tell her it is dangerous for her stay there alone. Just then, a huge bear walks towards the hut. The men are frozen in place as the bear walks up to the woman, allowing her to stroke its head. The woman says, "I will be looked after." Then hundreds of pairs of gold eyes shine out from the forest. Wolves have completely surrounded the hut. The woman lifts her hand, makes a slight sweeping motion and the wolves disappear. She whispers to the bear and it too departs. She says to the men, "Do you see? I will be fine."

The next day the men leave. The woman does not need to live in the hut. Like her predecessor, her body no longer needs physical sustenance. The hut has been prepared to be used one day when her successor arrives, but that will be many, many years from now.

T: I'm wondering if you want to do some work with this dream.
C: A starting point for me, is that it happened in a very significant time, when I had my hysterectomy. My life was totally changed at that time. If there was ever going to be a time for a dream like this, it was at this point, because it happened when I had shifted my whole life.
T: You made a bunch of other changes at that time too?
C: I realized I wanted to change my career. It took me a year to recover from surgery, but then I started my training as a therapist. It was a really significant point, deciding I could no longer stay in the same career. And I was coming to terms with my infertility, and starting to question my life purpose. It all swirled into that point: if I'm not going to be a mom, then what am I going to be? This dream arrived in response, it seemed to be telling me what my life was going to do. Because that woman was exactly the age I was when I had my hysterectomy. That's when I started my therapy training program. I just made that connection now.
T: The training, she goes through a training … such a different kind of training though. In this dream it's like she gives up her entire life to it.
C: That's what I feel like. I feel like I am in a training for my own spirituality. It started with my therapist training program because that forces you to do your own personal work. That was just the beginning, just dipping my toe in this new world. My therapy work is always with me because it's my job. But if I had to say which one is bigger, it's always going to be the personal work. I am now getting to a place where I can feel I am giving up everything – she left her family and that parallels me leaving India. But it's not actually the physical leaving of your family. To do the work, you have to emotionally leave them before you can reconnect with them in a different way. I think that's more what it's talking about because this spiritual work asks for a certain

detachment. Not in a cold way; it's sort of liking breaking the old patterns you've taken on because of ancestral and family ties. To be able to do my work, I have to disconnect from them.

T: To make a break and a clean start?

C: Or that I'm not that. Because I've identified so much with my family and culture, and to become who I'm becoming, I can't identify with that anymore because it's not really who I am. To go into that complete stillness is a letting go of all of these things that I've identified with. I'm leaving the world to grow into this place I'm growing into. The dream is giving me the story of what I'm going through.

T: Yes, it does feel like an entire life's journey is mapped out in this dream. It has an epic quality to it. You can see the pieces that relate to where you were when you had the dream. As a metaphor for your life, you're further down the road but not at the end.

C: No, nowhere near the end, because I see the end as being complete detachment from the world and finding the next person to give this wisdom to. I'm still in the process of letting go of the world and still learning. And even the thought of being in the world that the animals represent, that frightens me right now … But the funny thing is that at the same time I have a longing to be in that deeply, private wild space and in complete communion with everything.

T: So one thing I'm curious about is, who is this old woman? I'm wondering if you could visit the part of the dream where you see her.

C: (pause) I keep getting that she's me. She's obviously a different aspect. There's the me who is experiencing this right now and then she must be the crone, the big aspect, my wisdom self … I just don't get that she's that separate.

T: She's not that separate, she's an aspect of you that's older and wiser, and a teacher.

C: And yet she's separate too in some sort of way. There's a part of me that's her and there's an external part too. That part is not understandable, not a concept that would ever be known by this self, do you know what I mean?

T: I do. It's one of those enduring mysteries that you can't know. Here and now, there are many things you just can't know.

C: And she's one of them. It feels like there's a lineage that's being shown. So even when my life is over, there is a lineage that's passed down and that stretches back for a long time.

T: And is it all passed along by women?

C: Yeah I think it's feminine. And that's interesting that you say that because the men were involved here too, they were the doers. It's not about man and woman, it's about masculine and feminine energy and the masculine coming in to do the stuff, get things done, and the woman are doing some other kind of work entirely.

T: And the men are not allowed to come back, there will be repercussions if they do. I'm curious about that.

C: I did see something at the time I had the dream – a man trying to get somewhere. If he was on a mountain trail, he'd slip off. He just wouldn't be able

How Dreams Enlarge Us 125

to come back to that place. Whatever that place is and whatever its purpose is, it's protected. And I don't think it's because she's doing something overly secretive. I think it's because .... What is it...? It's something to do with having to stay purely feminine.

T: Right. And it sounds like there's a bit of a question ... you're chosen, the woman is chosen even though she has not had children. Is it some connection with the feminine ability to create life, and ... ?

C: Yeah, and when she held her hand and read all of the experiences that she'd had, the old woman felt she had gone through all the maternal stuff without having had children. She felt like a mother does. The word that comes up then is creative, she's still got creative energy. To her, that seems important.

T: There has to be this maternal/creative aspect to her, and that's necessary to be chosen. You don't have to have had literal children, you just need to have the sense of what that's about.

C: It feels like a really intense ability to completely feel and to love like that. And she has experienced it. She's had all the experiences needed to be able to open herself to that extent.

T: Because you couldn't do this training without that capacity, is that the idea?

C: Yeah it feels like that. And I just come back to my own life then, and right up to the age I was when I went through a whole heap of stuff ... with the arranged marriage and all the shit that happened, it was all kind of intense. I had a broken engagement, then the marriage to my first husband in India, and then the going-away ceremony and all the different sari changes, and I've just been back home to sort through all the pictures to do with that.

T: Such an involved ritual, and I see such a look of disgust.

C: There are so many photos of my life, and they have nothing to do with my current husband. So as I went through all these photos, I had to almost relive everything. And then to throw them away, I had no choice, I couldn't bring them all with me. It was a really difficult day.

T: Oh my goodness, you just did this ...

C: It made me realize, wow, I've been through a hell of a lot. It was all really emotional and there was a lot of horrible stuff that happened with the broken engagement and having to go back to India.

T: I can only imagine.

C: I'm a really private person, and I am just realizing how many public ceremonies I've endured where I was the centre of attention and having all of these demands: poked and prodded and pinned and dressed and preened and ugh, just not my idea of a good time. That was hell and so this 42-year-old woman in this dream and me have both experienced this powerlessness, and having to shut ourselves down completely to cope, and then re-open ourselves to love. And a lot of that happened with my animals. They were like my children. I showered them and lavished them with all of me, and I went through grief as I lost each one. By 42 I felt like I had lived many lives. So that really resonates with the 42 year old woman in my dream and when that woman held her hand. No wonder she accepted her, she had to. I thought yes, I have no doubt she is ready to begin this training. And what's interesting is she thinks as well, yes, I'm ready ... and she's not. (laughter). I can now sit here and laugh at her naiveté.

T: She thought, yes I'm ready for this, and she had no idea.

C: She had no idea. And so here's me today recalling my own sense at 42 of starting the therapy training thinking I knew all this stuff, and oh god, I had no idea what I was embarking on. Even the experiences from there to now have been earth-shattering. But this time it's been different because this time it has been on my own terms.

T: Right it was your own choice, and that's so different.

C: Yes, now I'm consciously training. That parallels the dream too. This next phase of my life is conscious training and involvement. And one of the things that I've been studying in spirituality is that you don't have to die to evolve. You can do it here. But to do that you do have to die in a way by letting of all your attachments. That was something I was contemplating as well, that if I died, I would let go of everything, including saying goodbye to my family, a sort of separation where you can be with them, still love them, but you don't need them. You are like a clear plate, and that's true freedom ...

If the ultimate goal is freedom, that's the wild place too. It's so interesting to me to have that wild animal place in the dream. It's where I feel torn in half right now because one of the things I'm struggling with the most is self-trust. So if I'm going to be walking in the forest on my own, I would be scared of wild animals. And yet I want nothing more than to be walking in the forest, completely wild and free. I want that equally as much as I'm afraid. So there's this longing, but I'm afraid at the same time and I can't reconcile those two pieces. I want to allow everything to be as it is, so if I'm going to die walking in the forest, okay ... I haven't gotten to that point yet.

T: So I'm wondering if you can enact this part of the dream, where you are in the forest, and the men are preparing to leave. The men are representing the fear in the dream I guess, they are fearing for your safety ... see if you can walk into the dream, into the place where the bear shows up, and just be the woman who is being with the bear. Just go back in there, and notice the feelings, sensations, thoughts, and whatever comes ...

C: She loves the bear. Because she is so connected to everything, she knows the bear, trusts the bear.

T: She knows it, trusts it, is connected with it. And the bear can sense that it seems.

C: Because she's so connected, she can sense everything. She has another sense in addition to the five senses and with that she can feel everything – the bear, the trees, the hut, the ground and everything. She can feel their fear. She is completely open.

T: If you can even be more identified with her. I mean using first person, but only if it feels natural, don't force it. See if you can find your way deeper into her so it would be natural to say, "I feel everything, I feel the bear, I love the bear ... just see if you can get there ... and let me know ...

C: I can feel it. I am her ...

T: So you're there. So from there I wonder, when you step deeper into the dream, what that's like?
C: (long silence) When you're her, you are in the expanded place.
T: So you're everything?
C: Yeah, I'm everything.
T: Is that how it is that you don't need any sustenance?
C: Because she doesn't have a body.
T: So you don't have a body. You just appear as though you do to the men?
C: There's a subset of her that's a body, a little droplet. She has a body but she's actually everywhere.
T: So that explains how the wolves come and go.
C: They were there anyway. It was more of a demonstration. Showing them, I'm fine. The whole thing was just to show them that there is nothing to fear.
T: So with that, coming back into your own sense of self, taking that, "I have nothing to fear here," can you have some of that for yourself? Is it possible to take some of that with you?
C: It's so hard to be in this world and … it's like what I need is to … I'm getting some information here. When I don't take time for myself, and when I don't get enough silence, then I get sucked into too much of being in the body and the fears that come with it. It's funny, there's a whole lot of information being given from this expanded place saying you need to take heaps more time in silence by yourself or you are always going to be struggling. This journey isn't going to happen if you don't take time for yourself.
T: So you need to take way more time for yourself in silence.
C: I've been doing token things and it's not working. The fears take hold. The more time I take in my body, the more I'm not taking the time to be empty and expanded, the fears have more opportunity to take root and grow.
T: It's like the soil is your solid body where they can take root.
C: That's so good, the solid body has soil in it and the fears take root. When I clear, they can't germinate. There's nothing for them to hold on to. What's been happening for the last little while is that I have not taken time out and one of the reasons I don't is because I compare myself to other people. They tend to have very busy lives, and I'm thinking I'm not doing half of what they are and I should, but I keep forgetting I can't compare myself to other people.
T: So it's really important for you to remember that.
C: Yes, and that this journey is a very private journey. The way it works for me is that I need lots of time by myself, and one of the things I have to do is dislodge my mom's voice saying, you're lazy. That's been a lifelong battle because to do nothing is to be lazy.
T: So there's that early indoctrination that you can't just be still and quiet, that's not an acceptable way to spend your time. But in fact when you get into that expanded place like the woman who is at the end of that journey, it's very clear to you what needs to happen.
C: Yes it's very clear. There needs to be a lot of time in silence.
T: It's like the hut is a metaphor for being off in the wilderness by yourself in a way?

C: It is. The hut feels like heaven, to be in the woods by myself but then there's that fear. There it is, that feeling ... And then there's another voice that says it doesn't matter, so what? It's all okay. Then I remember that, (a sigh, a visible shift), it's all okay.

T: So right there, there's that easing, it's all okay.

C: It's all okay, and then everything relaxes.

T: I see the change that just happened: your shoulders dropped, your body settled.

C: (long pause) It's really interesting, I've just been two weeks away and I had no time to myself, none. The only time I had any hours to myself was the time I spent was sorting through those old photos, and that wasn't ...

T: Not exactly still and quiet, that was like a whole journey of its own.

C: So I'm exhausted now. I see that just doesn't work for me.

T: You can't do that to yourself. You can't take that much time without some solitude or you suffer greatly.

C: So now I realise that to take time out, I need to stop all client work and I also need to stop everything else, and I need to do that two times a year. I didn't do that at all this year.

T: So you need to take complete chunks of time where you are doing the equivalent of going way off where no one can find you and sitting in a hut by yourself, or some version of that, or literally maybe ...

C: Yeah it almost becomes non-negotiable if this is my path. And my body is telling me this is my path because if I don't do the things along this path, I get sick.

T: It's not allowing you to make other choices, it's just saying how do you want to do this: kicking and screaming or do you want to come quietly?

C: That's exactly it! It's telling me that, what you just described so perfectly (laughter). Shall we do this quietly or ...

T: Or shall we have a scene? (mutual laughter) Wow so this is really affirming, I can hear that it comes from very deep in your soul. I don't use that word lightly, but this is what your calling is.

C: It is, yeah. There is no doubt. And the other thing that struck me when you just said that is that this calling is not public. You're the only one who knows this much about me. There's one other friend who is sort of on a similar path, so it's great to have her to be alongside on this journey. But otherwise, even my husband doesn't understand this, because it's not something you can talk about. It's incredibly private and will never be public even after I'm dead. So I think when she goes into the forest, and says to the men, you can't come back here that also speaks to how incredibly private it is.

T: That inner journey is, by definition, solo.

C: Yeah, it's solo. My family wouldn't understand it if I tried to put it in the most basic language and I don't have any desire to tell anybody.

T: It doesn't seem like you can. As much as you're telling me about it and I'm with you, I think about the way the real information is transmitted, and it is telepathically via their holding hands, as if there isn't really a way to say a

lot of things that get passed down, even if you wanted to. Like it's beyond articulating.
C: It's a private inner journey that can't be shared.
T: You can talk about it like we're doing but it's not the same as walking into the woods with you. That's your journey. It's a long journey away in the forest, and separate.
C: Where I live is very forested too. When we found that house that we live in, one of the attractions is the five big cedar trees, and there's a forest within walking distance. So when I moved away from my home country, I came to my forest, so that's a kind of parallel too, that Canada has that wildness I crave.
T: It does, it has the bears and the wolves and the forest and the mountains, and all of those things that you describe in your dream.
C: There's something here in Canada that holds me.
T: That gives you the space and the freedom … the freedom to just be. This dream, if it's a map of your life and your spiritual path in particular, it seems like something to really carry with you, and to keep revisiting. It feels like the things that you got from it are profound and it is also saying the same things that you know and are wanting.
C: It does, it's telling me what I'm wanting, it totally does.
T: It seems like if it is permission you need, there is a lot of permission in here, and not just that but such an honour to be chosen. You have to pass the test and have the right emotional experience and make-up, and from there you have to separate yourself from the world, which is the challenging bit right now it seems. Then there's a whole bunch of training that happens off-camera, which is appropriate, and then there's a place where you're supposed to pass this along. So we're in the off-camera part maybe.
C: And it's been gruelling. It feels like my body is going through challenges. There's been illnesses and fatigue, and beyond fatigue. All my stuff has been coming up for dealing with and letting go, and this huge amount of trust and self-acceptance being called for. It's a journey of coming to terms with yourself and letting go of all this crap that you thought you were.
T: That's a tall order for anyone.
C: I realize how much I've clung to stuff and anything I put my mind to, I hold on to. I want to be a good therapist and a good friend and it's all because I'm trying to boost myself up so I can feel good about myself. And then I need to try and dismantle all that because it doesn't serve me in the end.
T: So if I could suggest something, just from your dream. When you embody that expanded place, all those problems you describe, they seem to go away.
C: Yes they do. It's really lovely place to be. Sometimes before I start sessions, I go into that place to clear myself before I see people but when I'm busy then I can't.
T: Yeah, so I'm suggesting you spend more time there. I've just watched what you do. The minute you deeply enter into the wise woman part of you or the woman who is at the end of her training and patting the bear, those other things seem really insignificant.

C: You're right. It's been really helpful to talk to you about this. It's not something I can talk about.
T: Is there anything else in the dream that feels like it needs attention?
C: No it feels complete.

Observations and Commentary

This conversation can stand alone, but I will offer a few observations. First, I noticed that there were a couple of times when the dreamer gleaned more information from the dream than she already had, and those were specifically the times when she embodied the old wise woman and stepped into direct experiential contact with the dream. Second, I would note that as the dreamworker, sometimes the only thing needed is to reflect and describe what is already there in the dream. I have found that many times, the dream's message or story seems so obvious from the outside that there is no reason to offer such information. Yet hearing it back moves the dreamer forward, as if they were hearing it for the first time. We are often surprisingly blind to aspects of our own dreams, even stunningly obvious messages. So as the dreamworker, it is useful to simply play back what you hear and to ask about the places that seem unexplored by the dreamer. Don't assume the dreamer knows anything about their dream.

Further commentary concerns the somatic shifts that occurred in the process of discussing the dream. At one level, the dream discussion included attention to the anxiety threaded through the dreamer's life, and it was important to underscore the moment when the dreamer's body relaxed into a different state as she envisioned being off in a hut in the woods alone. The other tangible shift occurred as she embodied the wise old woman. She entered a clear open space that seemed like a powerful resource. If, as current brain research suggests, we need to trod new neural pathways over and over to make them more of an automatic part of our experience, it helps to revisit, and re-embody those places in therapy that bring welcome shifts.

Dreams as Preparation for Death: Facing the Sabretooth

Dreams that enlarge us in some way seem most often to lead the dreamer in a spiritual direction. Hillman (1979) wrote that all dreams are ultimately a preparation for death, and much has been written on this topic (e.g., Bulkeley & Bulkeley, 2005). Research into dreams of the dying shows that they tend to be more vivid and also more comforting than typical dreams. I will provide one example of such a dream from my practice to illustrate how initially terrifying and ultimately helpful such dreams can be.

A man I'll call John dreams he is walking with his daughter in an underground station after the world as we know it has been destroyed by a major disaster. Two women ahead open a door and release a sabre-tooth tiger that instantly devours them and then comes after him. His only concern is for his daughter. He runs with her to a door, and once she is through it, he closes it and turns to face certain death. The tiger pounces.

As he tells the dream, he is sweaty and flushed, but he says the feeling around it is not one of fear but more of resigned acceptance. His felt sense of contacting the tiger is in the middle of his chest, a collapsing heaviness. He says the tiger is enormous, sandy-colored, and that it feels primordial, archetypal. In the dream, John feels powerless, as though confronted by fate or destiny, a sense that this is simply how things are and it's nonnegotiable. He says, "When you come face to face with that, you're done."

Interestingly, in the dream, there is no sound, no eye contact, and no real fear or any other strong feeling despite the urgency of the action in the dream. Even in the dreamwork, the feelings are not intense or frightening, and although it is tempting to say this man is repressing those feelings, I know him to be someone very willing to face whatever comes his way. He reports a sense that once he has made sure his daughter is safe, there is no hurry, no goal or destination.

The dream is very alive, and John can see it and relive it in incredible detail, down to the type of doorknob and exact texture of the metal handrail on the stairs. He speaks of his strong father energy: the instinctual urge to save his child even if it means sacrificing himself. There is no hesitation in this. He also feels how very small he is in relation to the universe and how at his small level, he will do his best to save his own, though the success of even that feels uncertain.

He feels the impersonal nature of what he calls the higher power, a sense that it's not really concerned with what he calls "my mustard seed of a life." There is acceptance in this; it does not feel defeatist. Reflecting on the dream helped John shift his relationship with the process of aging and ultimately dying, something he had been worried about. The dream, by bringing him directly into contact with all of that, paradoxically brought him some comfort, a step closer to acceptance of his inevitable demise. He was grateful for making a tangible connection with massive and timeless force that will ultimately consume him.

References

Bulkeley, K. (2016). *Big dreams: The science of dreaming and the origins of religion.* London: Oxford University Press.

Bulkeley, K. & Bulkeley, P. (2005). *Dreaming beyond death: A guide to pre-death dreams and visions.* Boston, MA: Beacon Press Books.

Hillman, J. (1979). *The dream and the underworld.* New York, NY: HarperPerennial.

Kuiken, D., & Sikora, S. (1993). The impact of dreams on waking thoughts and feelings. In A. Moffitt, M. Kramer, & R. Hoffman (Eds.), *The functions of dreaming*, (pp. 419–476). Albany, NY: State University of New York Press.

14 Transformation

Applying Neuroscience to Dreamwork

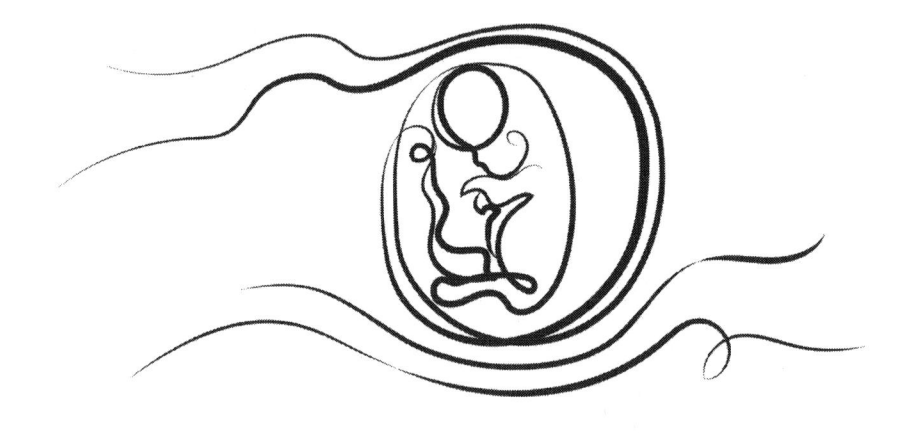

I've dreamt in my life dreams that have stayed with me ever after, and changed my ideas: they've gone through and through me, like wine through water, and altered the colour of my mind.

Emily Brontë

This chapter pulls together much of what we have discovered on the journey so far and proposes a model of dreamwork guided by our current understanding of the neurobiology of both dreaming and of transformational change. I will begin by summarizing an updated view of the unconscious and dreaming in light of current neuroscience. I will then offer a very brief and selective synthesis of how dreams might contribute to memory reconsolidation, how memory reconsolidation facilitates transformation, and how these two phenomena might work together in a clinical setting. I suggest that dreams can provide an important avenue for therapists to facilitate emotional memory reconsolidation. Because there has been a decided advance in our knowledge of these processes over the past decade or two, it is now possible to understand more clearly how new learning and change happen during the various stages of sleep, giving us a more sure-footed approach to transformational dreamwork. The chapter will conclude with a clinical example to ground these ideas in practice.

Dreams and an Updated Definition of the Unconscious

The working model of the unconscious has undergone significant revision in the past two decades. One of the world's leading cognitive neuroscientists, Gazzaniga (1998) proposed the idea of an "adaptive unconscious," which is conceived of as a complex and extensive network of neural processors that evaluate, calculate and respond to situations completely outside of our awareness. Far from the Freudian view of the unconscious as a seething cauldron of primitive and unacceptable desires, our automatic responses are now seen as generally adaptive and pervasive. Gazzaniga has suggested that fully 99 percent of our cognition is unconscious – or *implicit* (a better word for those impulses that happen outside of awareness since "unconscious" implies we are not just unaware, but not even awake).

If Gazzaniga is correct, there may be no such thing as free will, and cognitive scientists are now suggesting this is the case. What feels like a conscious decision on our part is actually our justification of an action after the fact. Gazzaniga (2012) said

> free will is an illusion … neuroscience, with its ever-increasing mechanistic understanding of how the brain enables mind, suggests that there is no one thing in us pulling the levers and in charge. It's time to get over the idea of free will and move on.

He said our brain is learning all the time, making increasingly better decisions about the best ways to behave. "That is what our brain is for and what it does. It makes decisions based on experience, innate biases, and mostly without our conscious knowledge. It is beautiful to understand how that happens."

Another way to say this is, "action precedes reflection." Bargh and Morsella (2008) suggest it is probably a good thing that our behavioral impulses do not come from our consciously-directed will.

> Contemporary social cognition research on priming and automaticity effects have shown the existence of sophisticated, flexible, and adaptive unconscious behavior guidance systems. These would seem to be of high functional value, especially as default behavioral tendencies when the conscious mind, as is its wont, travels away from the present environment into the past or the future. It is nice to know that the unconscious is minding the store when the owner is absent.

The authors go on to point out that in the rest of the natural world, unconscious processes are the rule, not the exception. While the human capacity to articulate and manipulate information is the most highly developed of any species, "this consciousness is not necessary to achieve the sophisticated, adaptive, and intelligent behavioral guidance demonstrated in the emerging priming literature. Unconscious processes are smart and adaptive throughout the living world."

Dreaming can be seen as a phenomenon that gives us a picture of our adaptive unconscious, and as such, dreams are an extremely valuable source of information for psychotherapists. Efrat Ginot (2015) wrote that dreams are highly significant as an "enacted expression of unconscious processes." She describes our emerging understanding of the REM phase of sleep where dreaming is most predominant and creative as "engaged not in simple consolidation of new/recent memory, but in processing associative memories." We also know that, for the most part, the material our dreams process is charged with emotion. Neural imaging shows us that during REM sleep and dreaming, our higher cortical processes are dampened down, and our limbic system is more active even than when we are awake.

Ginot said that because dreams are in part a result of limbic activity and compromised cognitive functioning they offer

> great therapeutic opportunities. Very often, more than the remembered content, the affect resurrected in dreams is significant for the possibility of change. As often experienced in treatment, the intense emotions that are revealed in dreams seem to provide one of the most direct accesses to what lies underneath; the emotional glue that holds a self-system together.

Operating from a modern psychoanalytic perspective, Ginot views dreams as an echo of a person's various *self-systems* reflecting the idea that our personalities are a collection of various states that we seamlessly slip in and out of depending on what our life situation calls for.

> Viewing all parts of a dream as echoing different self-systems can also give us an important glimpse into the patient's different unconscious systems and how they relate to each other or how internally split they are. Together with all other enacted manifestations of unconscious processes, *dreams open a window into what is hidden but still expressed.* (emphasis added)

You may or may not ascribe to current psychoanalytic theory (although dream elements as expressive of self-states is a concept worth exploring). Regardless, the main sentiment Ginot is expressing is that our updated understanding of the pervasiveness of unconscious processes and the role of dreams in opening a window into our implicit emotional worlds has increased the importance of attending to dreams in clinical practice.

> The emerging models of our dreaming lives strengthen their clinical relevance. Dreams can no longer be thought of as simply carrying repressed or dissociated memories or as a defense against unpleasant instincts. As part of always active brain/mind processes, they allow us, however strangely, to peek into unconscious processes as interpreted, recalled and retold by our conscious self.
>
> (Ginot, 2015)

Emotional Memory Reconsolidation: A Cause for Optimism

It used to be thought that emotional memories were not malleable, but the discovery of the processes behind emotional memory reconsolidation (Lane et al., 2015) has changed this view. Current evidence suggests the brain is more resilient and capable of changing and healing than previously thought, even later in life. This is a cause for optimism because now that we know something about the specific mechanisms of change, we can attempt to engineer our therapy processes to engender such changes. The beauty of this kind of change, which can take place in basic neural structures (at the synaptic level), is that once it has taken root, the test of success is that clients maintain the changed behavior *automatically and without effort*. This is not the white-knuckling kind of change that reverts back to its former patterns under stress.

Implicit emotional patterns are malleable, and can permanently transform into more up-to-date patterns, but only under the right circumstances. It used to be thought that long-term emotional memory was indelible because it was stored in synapses, in the basic structures of the brain. But Lee and colleagues (2004) have shown that if certain conditions are met, the synapses will destabilize, making revision of fear memory possible without reinforcing the original memory. According to Ecker, Ticic and Hulley (2012), the keys to unlocking the emotional brain involve clear, repeatable steps: (1) First, the client must identify and *experience* the existing implicit core belief system. Implicit emotional beliefs often have child-like reasoning attached to them because they were formed so early in life; the embodiment of such beliefs can feel strange and counter to logic, but still unshakeable. (2) Second, with that childlike belief alive and embodied, the client must experience an incompatible or contrasting sense, something that could not possibly be true at the same time. The contrasting feelings must be experientially real, and decisively felt. The disconnect this juxtaposition causes in the person's mind and body destabilizes the synapses involved in the memory network that holds this emotional belief pattern. (3) If over the next five hours (the time frame is quite specific), the newer learning is reinforced, it will stick. It will not just cover over the old information, but will actually replace it. Ecker and colleagues state that the resulting change will be transformational, rather than incremental. *It will last and will not require thought or effort to sustain.*

This is something to keep in mind when working with trauma. The traumatic events themselves are not the important focus. The process, and an open curiosity should be directed to the beliefs that arose out of the traumatic events with the understanding that fear generalizes. For example, people who suffered from chronic neglect in childhood often develop the belief that no one is *ever* there for them. Feeling deeply into the experience of having even one person consistently show up for them has the potential to shift this long-standing emotional pattern. This is why falling in love can be transformational. Implicit emotional beliefs are not generic, however, but quite specific. They must be retrieved from the body rather than speculated about with the mind for the change process to initiate.

Such beliefs and their opposites are often referred to in dreams. Jung was the first to notice this pattern. He found it so pervasive that he developed his theory of dreams as compensation around this idea. Although many early theories about dreams have been successfully challenged, this one persists and is incorporated into many current theories that suggest dreams bring new information and have the potential to transform our long-held emotional beliefs based on current experience. Therefore, dream material can be a rich source of experiential information to use as a base for facilitating memory reconsolidation within the process of psychotherapy.

This relatively new information about what engenders change in implicit emotional memory provides some sense of what to listen for when processing areas in a person's life that they wish to change. Good questions to explore do not refer to the issue or symptoms themselves, but rather to the beliefs about the world a person holds with respect to the presenting issue. It is helpful to inquire into ways these beliefs can be challenged in light of the client's current life situation, or in light of the novel experiences inherent in the therapy relationship. Ecker and his colleagues (2012), who have made the theory behind emotional memory reconsolidation widely available to clinicians, suggest that dreamwork is an effective method for uncovering and transforming implicit belief systems.

Doing What Dreams Do, Only Better

This section describes how we can take a dream and by focusing on it, assist in the very processes that dreams are implicated in – those of emotional memory reconsolidation and emotional regulation. Over time, dreams appear to help take the emotional charge out of challenging memories while enabling us to retain the information we need to make more adaptive decisions in the future. Dreamwork can augment and strengthen this process. And it can kick-start a 'failed' dreaming process that is not working as it should (as we demonstrated with dream rescripting treatments for PTSD nightmares).

One of the challenges of trying to engender emotional memory reconsolidation is that it can take quite a bit of detective work to uncover an outdated emotional belief that was formed implicitly. Ideas about the nature of the world are often formed in childhood based on experiences from one's family of origin, and early beliefs are rarely explicit or called into question. Having no other frame of reference as very young children, we see our environment as simply how the world works, and the beliefs we pick up are a way of adapting to the emotional and relational world we found ourselves in. Dreams, however, can bring our emotional beliefs to life as metaphorical images we experience directly. They often represent novel information that contradicts what we believe. Such images are the keys that can unlock the process of emotional memory reconsolidation, updating and transforming how we respond to life situations in light of current experience.

Already, those who consistently work with dreams as part of their practice of psychotherapy have an intuitive understanding of how to work with dreams to bring about therapeutic change. Most invite their clients into a deeply experiential sense of the dream, a critical ingredient in the process. Dreams often have within them contrary elements that can be juxtaposed. To be more skillful and precise as dreamworkers, it is helpful to understand some of the mechanisms of sleep and dreaming that lead to new learning. In a series of two articles, Horton and Malinowski (2015a, 2015b), describe in detail existing research leading to a theory about the mechanics of emotion assimilation and memory consolidation in sleep and dreaming.

In the first article, on the transformation of autobiographical memory, the authors propose a model that suggests the nocturnal memory consolidation process "gives rise to dreaming" by breaking our memories into fragments and recombining the most salient elements into new experiences that are *hyperassociatively* linked to what the dreaming brain deems relevant from its vast store of existing information. In the process, the emotions that have tagged which specific elements from the day's experience are novel or important enough to remember, attenuate; they have done their job and can now fade. This theory potentially implicates dreaming in consolidating and reconsolidating (updating) our memories, and also suggests that the basic dreamwork steps of recalling and telling the dream can facilitate this adaptive process. I would add that beyond the telling of the dream, spending time with the dream images and emotions and allowing the associative process to continue while awake, can further facilitate the updating of memories in light of new information.

What do we dream about? Malinowski and Horton (2015a) present evidence that there are three main ways material from our waking lives is selected to feature in our dreams. The first is the emotional intensity of the experience, but not the valence. It used to be thought that we preferentially dream about negative experiences, but this has been revised (e.g. Schredl & Doll, 1998). The second selection criterion is the age of the experience: we often dream of what happened during the previous day, a common occurrence Freud named "day residue." More recently, it has been shown that we also tend to incorporate waking experiences from five to seven days prior into our dreams, the so-called *dream-lag effect* (e.g. Nielsen, et al., 2004). The third factor that determines what shows up in our dreams is the personal salience of recent events. The authors propose that during memory processing in sleep, the purpose of breaking apart memories and reconsolidating them with just those memory elements selected based on emotion, timing and relevance to the future, is to improve the future accessibility of key memory fragments in a variety of contexts. This is a potential explanation for the strangeness of dreaming – why our dreams pick up certain aspects of our recent experience and combine them with seemingly random events from the past.

In addition to explicating current evidence of how dreams relate to memory consolidation, Malinowski and Horton (2015b) surveyed theories of emotional assimilation in dreaming and found the main theories had the following in common: emotional processing in dreaming is iterative and takes place over time because it goes through a series of stages of memory activation and recombination before emotional adaptation is achieved. There are many variables affecting this complex process, including the nature of the emotional events being processed and the psychological nature of the dreamer. To summarize their argument in favor of viewing dreaming as, at least in part, an emotional assimilation process: we tend to dream more and recall more about emotional than neutral experiences, and we tend to adapt better to emotional experiences that we dream about. The authors also suggest that a healthy imagination is critical to the effectiveness of these processes. Healthy dreaming is creative, metaphorical and at times bizarre. These imaginative elements are exactly what is missing from the dreams of those suffering from PTSD, and it is the rekindling of imaginative capacities that appears to move the dreaming process in a healthier direction, reducing both nightmare frequency and PTSD symptoms (e.g. Krakow, et al., 2001; Ellis, 2016).

In the emotion assimilation model proposed by Horton and Malinowski (2015b), metaphor is seen as the vehicle by which this important dream function takes place. The idea that dreams are picture-metaphors depicting emotion (Hartmann, 2011) has gained wide acceptance. Dream metaphors tend to bring together widely disparate elements. They are also highly specific to the dreamer, and often make no sense until the dreamer's unique associations are explored. This is why standard dream dictionaries that claim to decipher the meaning of dreams are of very limited use. It is often necessary to spend time and understand the details of how a dream image might relate to the dreamer's life before the metaphorical language the dream is speaking can be understood. Not all dreams are characterized by mysterious metaphors that require exploration to decipher, but those that do are often highly creative and novel, and as such are seen by the authors as "particularly useful for making new discoveries."

The emotion assimilation theory of dreaming is complex, difficult to summarize and in some areas, is a work in progress because the research supporting aspects of the theory is incomplete or contradictory. In spite of this, taken as a whole, it is convincingly argued that dreaming reflects the complementary processes of emotional assimilation and long-term memory consolidation via a process that breaks waking life experiences into fragments that are recombined creatively in dreams using metaphor and hyperassociativity. They also suggest that dreams do their work whether we are aware of what we've dreamt or not, but that recalling and processing our dream material can strengthen these very processes.

At this point, dream researchers are still building the case that dreaming may reflect the processes of offline memory activation that lead to consolidation. There are compelling arguments to suggest that dreaming reflects and/or affects what and how we remember, but exactly how it does this is still both theoretical and speculative. The field is new, and the process it is trying to explicate is incredibly complex. Despite this, I believe that as clinicians, it helps us to be informed by the science, to extract the gist of what the most current research says about the nature of dreams. For example, it is useful to understand something of why the language of dreams is metaphoric, and how the neurochemical properties of the sleep stages associated with dreams alter the way we can think and remember (i.e. within dreaming, not very well).

In this chapter, I am suggesting that armed with a basic (and yes, speculative) understanding of the role of dreaming in emotional memory consolidation, we may be able to explore the dreams that clients bring to therapy in a way that facilitates or strengthens the helpful processes that dreams are already a part of; well-considered current theories suggest that dreams are implicated in the process of reducing the emotional charge of memories that have current relevance, and also in updating our store of memories to include current experience, better preparing us for what's next. This could also serve as a definition of what happens in psychotherapy. Not just the dreams themselves, but the dreamwork process within therapy can facilitate these emotional and memory updating processes. In addition, nightmare treatment research has shown that by using what we know about dreams in specific and thoughtful ways, we can repair sleep-dream-memory processes that are not working well, helping healthy dreaming to resume. I am grateful to all of the researchers who have made these processes more understandable and clinically relevant.

Dreamwork as More Art than Science

I am now going to turn from dream research and physiological theories about their nature, which are helpful in illuminating certain aspects of dreams, toward the dreams themselves. Ultimately, I believe dreams are best appreciated phenomenologically – through personal experience and reflection of how our own dreams impact us. And as therapists, we can extend this to working with the dreams of others. Dreams are a unique form of experience that relate to our personal lives, and beyond. Understanding the dreaming process is an ongoing challenge, and it is worthwhile to track current research. However, the act of *working* with dreams, both personally and professionally, remains more of an art than a science. It is good to keep in mind what we know of the specific mechanics of emotional memory transformation, but also to keep that understanding in the background so we can maintain the quality of presence needed to help guide our clients through an active experience of their dreams. Over time, clinicians who work consistently with dreams will develop an intuitive sense of where the dream has the most energy or information for the dreamer. My sense is that it is best to allow the conversation about dreams to flow and to avoid being too mechanical about it. This chapter represents an example of what McGilchrist (2009) suggests is the optimal way to use our brainpower: begin with the experience of the dream (mediated by the right hemisphere), consider the steps we need to facilitate therapeutic change as laid out in current research (mediated by the left hemisphere), and then switch back to an open-ended, reflective and creative mode to carry out the actual dreamwork. McGilchrist suggested this right-left-right movement is how our brains are meant to be used.

As you have seen throughout this book, the dreams themselves contain transformative elements. Dream exploration gains its therapeutic value when we accompany and guide the dreamer into an experiential way of reliving the dream, encouraging them to feel their way back into the dream's landscape of associations and its intricate web of connections with waking life, and possibly beyond.

This takes time, and a meandering nondirective approach that may feel out of step with current emphases on goal-directed and evidence-based interventions. I am hoping these forays into the science behind dreaming will satisfy the need for dream therapists to justify dreamwork from a logical perspective and eliminate some of the bias against dreamwork we so often encounter. My goal here is to place dreamwork on a solid theoretical foundation so it frees you up as a dreamworker to explore in the open-ended way that dreams respond to.

Clinical Examples of Transformational Dreamwork

What I have noticed about the process of memory reconsolidation is that theories of psychotherapy incorporated its basic elements well before the neuroscience underlying the process was discovered. The trend in dreamwork toward greater experiential practices is an example of how therapists intuit and/or learn by experience to use methods that engender change. In addition, Jung's notion that dreams are compensatory, and Gendlin's bias control are two ways dreamwork brings about an experiential juxtaposition that can cause significant shifts in the dreamer's store of emotional memory. To cite one example, from the beginning of this book, my dream about being swept into a whirlpool and reaching out into thin air was a frightening feeling forever altered by the entirely unexpected sensation of someone grabbing my hand and letting me know they were with me. I could feel my whole system recalibrating in response to that. Another example in the book is the lion dream, in particular the responses the dreamer has after I ask her to *become* the lion. Once she had entered into the perspective of the animal she had so greatly feared, her entire response to the dream changed, and she could feel how the energy it released would continue to do its work without her conscious effort.

Another example of memory reconsolidation at work is shown in the dreamwork with the Grateful Dead dream. Initially, the dreamer is terrified of being shot by "Jack," the man who in waking life had been abusive and was now aware of where she worked. In the dreamwork, this fear was juxtaposed by the feelings of safety I encouraged her to sink into very deeply. There were at least two safe places in the dream to draw from: memories of her first love, and also being with a group of like-minded people on the bus who prevent Jack from harming her. In a later part of the session, I ask the dreamer to "be" Jack for a minute, another form of juxtaposition; she feels how hollow and sick he is, before we move on to the part of the dream where she is safe on the bus.

There is a palpable release of tension in the course of working with the dream, and this is sustained, which is the hallmark of a successful memory reconsolidation process. The dreamer reported that prior to the dreamwork, she felt very anxious in general, and especially going to work. After the dreamwork, the fear was no longer present. She said, "I'm not holding the charge anymore." She could walk into work without her usual worried pausing at the threshold, and this was not a conscious, but an effortless, automatic action reflective of a structural change in the nature of her fear memories. Interestingly, in her subsequent dream, she confronts Jack and he apologizes, which is further evidence of change. I believe such dream changes are significant and authentic reflections of clinical change because they happen without conscious volition. The dreamwork also shifted the way the dreamer holds the memories about Jack, with more of a focus on her friends coming to her rescue and her desire to cultivate community in her life.

The "new was"

In the preceding example, the client arrives at a new vantage point. From there, she views the past differently, but also, paradoxically, with a sense that it has always been that way. Gendlin (1984), called this the "new was." He viewed feelings, thinking, actions and words all primarily as lived experience in the body, and each bodily event as implying what comes next. He called this "carrying forward" and said,

> In therapy we change not into something else, but into more truly ourselves. Therapeutic change is into what that person really 'was' all along… it is a second past, read retroactively from now. It is a new 'was' made from now.

From this *new was*, steps come that change one's conception of the past entirely. The change is not just a current one, but a shift that ripples through our entire store of memory revising many things accordingly.

There is room here to think about state-dependent memory, something I encounter frequently in working as a psychotherapist. To play with the above example, when the client feels afraid, the memories of Jack feel much more ominous and she recalls the worst ones. When she is less afraid, she may recall better times, such as her earlier relationship with her first love. This fear bias colors her perception of the world in general, and of relationships specifically. I believe that the elements of this dream were particularly salient and powerful tools for engendering lasting change in her sense of relational safety. It can be a challenge in psychotherapy to create deeply-felt juxtapositions necessary to revise emotional memory, but dreams provide ready-made and highly relevant material for this powerful transformation process.

Summary of Lessons from This Book: Why and How to Work with Dreams

With that, we have come to the end of this journey into the ways to work with dreams in therapy. I hope it has given you a sense of excitement about the prospect of working with the dreams your clients bring, as well as some good ideas about what to ask and how to proceed. Ideally it marks the beginning, or the way forward to a further deepening of your relationship with the enduring mystery of the dream world.

While the science of dreaming is advancing steadily, and the case for working with dreams in clinical practice is stronger than ever as a result, there remains much about dreams that is ambiguous, controversial and/or a matter of debate.

It is part of what makes dreams attractive, the fact that we can never quite pin them down or say for certain what they are, where they come from or what, exactly, we should do in response to them. Increasingly, my sense is that, at the very least, we should pay attention to them, appreciate them, and allow their stunning ability to transport us into experiences beyond imagining to expand our horizons, and those of our clients.

The future of dreamwork seems promising, as research continues on many fronts, aided by dramatic advances in technology. Although it now seems out of reach, the idea that we could efficiently depict our dreams in moving images rather than words is one that could change the way we relate to dreams both in and out of therapy. There is also a growing interest among young people about dreaming, spurred by feature films like *Inception* that depict adventures in the realm of lucid dreaming. Although the psychotherapy profession is currently dominated by a paradigm that devalues dreamwork, I see evidence that this pendulum has begun to swing, and that there is hunger for the creative, playful, social and spiritual dimensions that dreams invite. As clinicians, paying attention to our dreams can bring both personal benefits, insight into our relationships with our clients, and a deeper understanding of how to navigate the dreams of others. In addition, dreamwork will enrich your own practice: it will be deeper, more imaginative, more effective, and more fun!

In Closing

This book began with the question, why work with dreams? It took you on a journey that included: my personal and clinical experience with dreamwork, my exploration of the world of dream research and its struggle with the challenge of determining the nature and function of dreaming, and finally, a tour of some new ideas I offer respectfully, aware they stand on the shoulders of many great thinkers and scholars. I have proposed that the common factors of modern Western dreamwork have shifted from a content to a process model, and that this has already shifted the way dreamwork is being done across modalities: away from analytical toward more experiential methods. Lastly, I have gathered current information about emotional memory reconsolidation from several fronts: neuroscience, psychotherapy theory and dream research, to propose a theory and method of experiential clinical dreamwork with the potential to facilitate transformational change.

All of this has been a tremendous journey of learning over the space of more than a year, taking me from Day of the Dead in a small Mexican town to the quaint shores of Swansea, Wales, and on numerous smaller journeys. I have attended conferences, workshops and dreamwork sessions of all types, both as a participant and facilitator. I've spoken with researchers, read volumes of papers, and sought feedback and clarification from many dream experts. Along the way I have learned much about the nature of dreams and in particular, how to apply this knowledge to working with dreams in clinical practice. My views have expanded and shifted during the time I have spent asking into the nature of dreams. I have marveled at their stunning intensity, creativity and humor. After all this, strangely, in some ways I feel less certain of my understanding of dreams than when I started, but I love that dreams remain an enduring mystery.

However, I do feel that I have adequately answered my initial question: why work with dreams? Their depth, richness and invitation to inner experiencing and exploration seem almost infinite. Helping clients touch into this depth can bring welcome change. Although at times, dreams can be intense and frightening, mostly, they seem to help. When we become skilled at facilitating our clients' relationship to their dreams, the dreams themselves appear to respond, to open further and become even more of a guiding light.

Embryo in the Water Dream

I'll leave you with one more dream session because it brings many of the water dream stories threaded through this book full circle. *The dreamer IS the water, and is seeing a person in a car, not panicked, in the driver's side of a vehicle sinking slowly into deep, dark water. Both the person in the car and the dreamer become aware of an embryo, up and to the left that is bathed in a shaft of light, and it's not clear whether the light is coming from or shining on the "ready-to-be-born" embryo that could be dog or human. The light is illuminating the way up and out. The person takes a deep breath, and is suddenly outside the vehicle scooping the embryo up and gently swimming to the surface. They call for help and everybody in the dream responds. The people on the water gently pull the person and embryo into their boat, and at this moment, the dreamer is no longer water, but the person being rescued. He is taken to shore, gently set down and tended to. The community's elder, or "person-of-age" is how the dreamer wanted to express it, accompanies the dream ego as they shift from dog to human, and with each shift, the dog becomes healthier, more vital. Then the person-of-age gives the dreamer an affirming nod and turns to attend to the embryo.*

In dreaming the dream on, we explored the mobilization of help as this was a deeply emotional place for the dreamer. There was such an expansive sense of support, he felt he could truly rest into it. We inquired into the fluid nature of the dream ego, quite literally fluid, the dreamer noted with a laugh, "it being water." The dreamwork process moved the central action in the dream forward, giving the dreamer the assurance that the embryo was going to survive and now was ready to be born.

References

Bargh, J. A., & Morsella, E. (2008). The unconscious mind. *Perspectives on Psychological Science*, 3(1), 73–79.
Ecker, B., Ticic, R. & Hulley, L. (2012). *Unlocking the emotional brain: Eliminating symptoms at their roots using memory reconsolidation.* New York, NY: Routledge.
Ellis, L. (2016). Qualitative changes in recurrent PTSD nightmares after focusing-oriented dreamwork. *Dreaming*, 26(3), 185–201.
Gazzaniga, M. (1998). *The mind's past.* Oakland, CA: University of California Press.
Gazzaniga, M. S. (2012). *Free will is an illusion, but you're still responsible for your actions.* In The Chronicle of Higher Education. Web http://chronicle.com/article/Michael-S-Gazzaniga/131167, downloaded 2019, posted 2012.

Gendlin, E. T. (1984). The client's client: The edge of awareness. In R. L. Levant & J. M. Shlien (Eds.), *Client-centered therapy and the person-centered approach. New directions in theory, research and practice*, pp. 76–107. New York, NY: Praeger.

Ginot, E. (2015). *The neuropsychology of the unconscious*. New York, NY: W. W. Norton.

Hartmann, E. (2011). *The nature and functions of dreaming*. New York, NY: Oxford University Press.

Horton, C. L. & Malinowski, J. E. (2015a). Autobiographical memory and hyperassociativity in the dreaming brain: Implications for memory consolidation in sleep. *Frontiers in Psychology*, 6:874.

Horton, C. L., & Malinowski, J. E., (2015b). Metaphor and hyperassociativity: The imagination mechanisms behind emotion assimilation in sleep and dreaming. *Frontiers in Psychology*, 6:1132.

Jung, C. G.; Aniela Jaffé (1965). *Memories, Dreams, Reflections*. New York, NY: Random House.

Krakow, B., Hollifield, M., Johnston, L., Koss, M., Schrader, R., Warner, T. D …. (2001). Imagery rehearsal therapy for chronic nightmares in sexual assault survivors with post-traumatic stress disorder: a randomized controlled trial. *JAMA*, 286, 537–545.

Lee, J. L., Everitt, B. J., & Thomas, K. L. (2004). Independent cellular processes for hippocampal memory consolidation and reconsolidation. *Science*, 304, 839–843.

Lane, R. D., Ryan, L., Nadel, L., & Greenberg, L. (2015). Memory reconsolidation, emotional arousal, and the process of change in psychotherapy. *Behavioral and Brain Sciences*, 38, 64 pp.

McGilchrist, I. (2009). *The master and his emissary: The divided brain and the making of the Western world*. New Haven, CT: Yale University Press.

Nielsen, T. A., Kuiken, D., Alain, G., Stenstrom, P., & Powell, R. A. (2004). Immediate and delayed incorporations of events in dreams: Further replication and implications for dream function. *Journal of Sleep Research*, 13, 327–336.

Schredl, M., & Doll, E. (1998). Emotions in diary dreams. *Consciousness and Cognition*, 7, 634–646.

Index

action steps prompted by dreams 11, 37
activation-synthesis theory 41
archetypes 25, 28, 34–35, 59, 121; *see also* "big dreams"; Jung, Carl Gustav
artistic depiction of dreams 35, 87–89; DreamsID 89–93; high-tech reproduction 93–94
associations to dreams 33, 35, 36, 52, 56, 67, 69, 70, 98, 114, 138, 139

bias control 22, 26, 35, 140
"big dreams" 10, 21, 59–60, 121–122; dream case studies 122–131; preparation for death 13, 31, 130–131
body dreamwork 99

cognitive-behavioral therapy 13
common factors research 29, 66, 67
compensatory dreaming 26, 35, 136, 140
complexes 26
continuity hypothesis 39
creativity of dreams 14, 51, 52, 138

daydreams 39–40
death: preparation for *see* "big dreams"
default mode network 41
depression 64
devaluing of dreams in Western culture 23, 25, 69, 94
diagnostic information from dreams 15, 63
dream case studies: bear in the kitchen 52–53; embryo in the water 143; facing the sabretooth 130–131; Gabby and the "holy trinity" 81–85; Grateful Dead 104–108; Honoré women 122–130; lion 114–120; perfect newborn 100–101; runaway jeep 54–56; underwater woman 53–54; woman in the mirror 71–78

"dream divide" 25, 31, 51–52, 60, 64; and bilateral brain 68–69, 139; clinical navigation of 66–70; dream case study 71–78
dream interview method 35, 55, 68
dream-life themes and phases 22; *see also* recurrent dreams
dream tending 97, 98
dream therapy: art more than science 139; and client engagement 12–13; client initiation of 11, 19; enriches psychotherapy 9–10, 13, 15; evidence base expanding 2–3, 8; exposure therapy vs. 17; research on benefits of 10–12, 138; and science of dreaming 38–39; underused by clinicians 2–3, 8, 11, 12, 20, 68, 140, 142
"dreamism" 60
dreamwork decision tree 70

embodied dreamwork *see* embodied imagination method; focusing approach; process work
embodied imagination (EI) method 67–68, 96–97
emotion assimilation model 137–138
emotional landscape of dreams 33
emotional memory consolidation *see* memory consolidation
emotional regulation 2, 3, 16, 42, 43
empathy 46
evolution of memory 44
existential dreams *see* impactful dreams
experiential methods 28, 30–31, 55, 137, 139; cognitive-experiential model 11, 37; exploring dream elements 33; interpretive approach eclipsed by 30, 66; re-entry of dreams 30, 36, 55, 83; *see also* embodied imagination method; focusing approach; process work

146 *Index*

finding help in dreams 36, 79–80; dream case study 81–85; manifestly helpful dreams 80; nightmares 80, 85–86, 104, 108–109; searching for positive elements 80, 85–86, 99, 108–109
FiveStar method 64
focusing approach 22, 28, 31, 32, 96, 99; dream case study 100–101; *see also* bias control; embodied dreamwork; finding help in dreams
free will 133
Freud, Sigmund 28; day residue 137; distortion of dream message 2, 41, 51; emotional regulation 16, 43; free association 33; interpretation of dreams 29; unconscious 133

generic dreamwork method 31–37; *see also* dreamwork decision tree
generic reformulation of dreams 35
Gestalt methods 28, 33
group dreamwork 11, 12, 30–31, 36–37, 68; dream case study 114–120; person-centered approach group incident process (PCAGIP) 113–114; projective dreamwork (Taylor) 113; Ullman group process 112, 113, 114–120; usefulness of 112–113

Hill method 31, 34, 37
hyper-associativity 40, 43, 137

imagery rehearsal therapy (IRT) 2, 12, 109
imaginative play 46
impactful dreams 10, 60, 122; *see also* "big dreams"
insight and personal growth 34
integral method 31
internal censorship bypassed in dreams 1, 10, 13–14, 17, 22, 51, 52
interpersonal neurobiology 2, 39
Introduction to the Psychology of Dreaming 29

Jung, Carl Gustav 2, 28; archetypes 25, 28, 34, 59, 121; artistic depiction of dreams 35, 88; "big dreams" 7, 59, 121; compensatory dreaming 26, 35, 136, 140; dreaming the dream forward 108; mythological interpretation 34, 59
Jungian therapy 2, 9, 28; depth psychology 97–98; *see also* embodied imagination method

life force in dreams 79–80, 98, 99, 101; *see also* finding help in dreams
lucid dreaming 12, 36, 39, 61–62, 110; and video gaming 93

memory consolidation 3, 16, 40, 110, 137; dream-lag effect 137; emotional memory consolidation 135–136; and emotional regulation 43; episodic memories 44; selectivity of dreams 52, 137; sleep-related performance enhancement 45–46
metaphor: central vs. connected dream images 53; dream case studies 52–56; emotion assimilation model 137–138; metaphorical interpretation of dreams 10, 13, 33–34, 50–51; physical basis of 49–50; ubiquity in language 50; vehicle for emergent meaning 51
mythological interpretation 34–35, 59

neurophysiology 44
"new was" *see* state-dependent memory
nightmares 60, 62; dream case study 104–108; as failure in dream function 16, 42, 104, 108, 136; finding help in 108–109; lucid dreaming as therapy 61, 93, 110; and posttraumatic stress disorder 2, 12, 15; usefulness of 103
night terrors 62
no-adaptive-purpose theories 41–42

plot structure analysis 35
polyphasic cultures 69
posttraumatic stress disorder (PTSD): change in dreaming patterns 15, 104; dreaming the dream forward 109–111; exposure and mastery 110–111; imagery rehearsal therapy 2, 12, 109; lucid dreaming as therapy 12, 61, 110; non-evolution of memories 44, 51, 64, 104, 138; recurrent dreams 63–64; *see also* nightmares
precognitive dreams 15, 63
premonitions *see* precognitive dreams
process work 97, 98–99
projection onto dreams 26, 30, 31, 36–37, 70, 113, 115; *see also* group dreamwork
psychoanalysis 2, 134
psychosis 64
PTSD *see* posttraumatic stress disorder

recalling dreams 21–22; dream journals 21; sketches 21, 22, 88

recurrent dreams 63–65; *see also* posttraumatic stress disorder
REM/dreaming distinction 40

self-analysis of therapists' dreams 20
sleep cycle 21, 23
sleep deprivation 23, 40, 63; REM/dream deprivation 24–25, 40; REM rebound 24
sleep paralysis 62–63
social sharing of dreams 22–23, 26, 34–35, 46, 69, 91, 94, 113
social simulation theory 46
spectrum of mental functioning 39–40
spiritual health and dream life 24–25
state-dependent memory 141

telling dreams 10, 30, 32–33; and dream re-entry 30

thermoregulation 40
threat simulation theory 42, 46
transcendent dreams *see* impactful dreams
transpersonal vs. wake-centric perspectives *see* "dream divide"

unconscious: adaptive unconscious 133–134; aspects of personality 14; collective 59, 98, 121; dreams as window on 134; expressed through art 35, 89; Freudian 133; messages from 99; projections 26
uplifting dreams 22, 36

video gaming and lucid dreaming 93

Working with Dreams and PTSD Nightmares 29

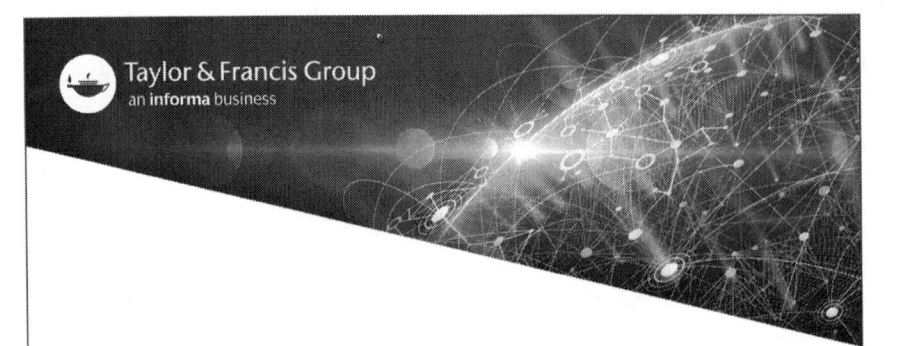